Rebecca West and the God That Failed

BY CARL ROLLYSON

Biographies

Marilyn Monroe: A Life of the Actress
Lillian Hellman: Her Legend and Her Legacy
Nothing Ever Happens to the Brave: The Story of Martha Gellhorn
The Lives of Norman Mailer
Rebecca West: A Saga of the Century
Pablo Picasso
Susan Sontag: The Making of an Icon (with Lisa Paddock*)*
Beautiful Exile: The Life of Martha Gellhorn
Marie Curie: Honesty in Science
To Be A Woman: The Life of Jill Craigie

On Biography

Biography: An Annotated Bibliography
Reading Biography
Essays in Biography
A Higher Form of Cannibalism? Adventures in the Art and Politics of Biography
Biography: A User's Guide (forthcoming)

Literary Criticism

Uses of the Past in the Novels of William Faulkner
The Literary Legacy of Rebecca West
Reading Susan Sontag
Female Icons: Marilyn Monroe to Susan Sontag

Film Criticism

Documentary Film: A Primer

Interviews

In Their Own Voices: Teenage Refugees from Eastern Europe Speak Out

Reference Works

Herman Melville A to Z (with Lisa Paddock)
The Brontës A to Z (with Lisa Paddock)
The Facts on File Encyclopedia of American Literature, Volume 3: The Modern Period and Postmodern Period From 1915
Where America Stands: What Americans Think and Need to Know About Today's Most Critical Issues (with Michael Golay)

Genealogy

A Student's Guide to Polish-American Genealogy (with Lisa Paddock)
A Student's Guide to Scandinavian-American Genealogy (with Lisa Paddock)

Edited by Carl Rollyson

Critical Survey of Drama, Second Revised Edition
Critical Survey of Long Fiction, Second Revised Edition
Notable British Novelists
Notable American Novelists
Notable Playwrights
British Biography: A Reader

Rebecca West and the God That Failed

✦

Essays

Carl Rollyson

iUniverse, Inc.
New York Lincoln Shanghai

Rebecca West and the God That Failed
Essays

Copyright © 2005 by Carl Rollyson

iUniverse books may be ordered through booksellers or by contacting:

iUniverse
2021 Pine Lake Road, Suite 100
Lincoln, NE 68512
www.iuniverse.com
1-800-Authors (1-800-288-4677)

ISBN-13: 978-0-595-36227-1 (pbk)
ISBN-13: 978-0-595-80672-0 (ebk)
ISBN-10: 0-595-36227-3 (pbk)
ISBN-10: 0-595-80672-4 (ebk)

Printed in the United States of America

Contents

PREFACE

After completing my biography of Rebecca West in 1995, I felt bereft. As my wife said, "Rebecca was such good company." I had already embarked on another biography, but Rebecca kept beckoning me. I felt there was more to say about her politics—a misunderstood part of her repertoire as reporter and novelist. And had I done justice to her enormous sense of fun and humor? I really regretted excising the portrait of her I wanted to put at the beginning of my biography. My editor kept cutting away at what he called my doorstop of a book. And then after years of waiting, I was sent her FBI file. I kept running into Rebecca, so to speak, when I was writing my biographies of Martha Gellhorn and Jill Craigie. Interviews in London often turned up people who had known West as well.

Thus piece by piece, I accumulated what is now another book about Rebecca West. This new collection tells the story of how my biography got written, of what it means to think like a biographer, and why West's vision remains relevant. She is one of the great personalities and writers of the modern age, and one that we are just beginning to comprehend.

INTRODUCING REBECCA WEST

This review of Selected Letters of Rebecca West, edited by Bonnie Kime Scott and published by Yale University Press will serve as a good introduction. Like many of my other West pieces, this one first appeared in The New Criterion.

Readers of *The New Criterion* may not need an introduction to Rebecca West. Her literature, life, and politics have been discussed in these pages on several occasions. Yet even those familiar with her biography and body of work will find startling new material in this superbly edited collection of her correspondence. Although West was always outspoken, her letters reveal a behind-the-scenes candor that provides refreshing insight into her reporting on the suffragists, the New Deal, Yugoslavia, the Nuremberg trials, the Cold War, Communism and much more. Devotees of her great novels, *The Fountain Overflows* and *The Birds Fall Down*, will be granted a new awareness of the autobiographical and historical roots of her fiction.

Born in 1892, West remembered the Silver Jubilee of Queen Victoria and the sight of soldiers returning from the Boer War. This collection begins with a letter to *The Scotsman* (October 16, 1907), in which a fourteen-year-old West (then still using her family name, Cicily Isabel Fairfield) expresses her strong opinions on the subjection of women. A feminist and a socialist, West was also attracted to the stage. Indeed, her pen name is that of Ibsen's heroine in *Rosmersholm*. At a very early age, in other words, West was already an accomplished writer and a figure bound to attract the public eye.

Short, dark featured, opinionated, West did not seem to theater directors the kind of ingénue they could fit into their productions. Abandoning a theatrical career, she began writing for journals such as *The New Freewoman* and *The Clarion* and was adopted by literary lights such as Ford Madox Ford, who admired her keen intelligence and astringent style. West came to Ford's attention when she had reviewed one of his novels rather negatively. Similarly, H.G. Wells took her up after she ridiculed his view of women in *Marriage*, one of his "conversation" novels. In both cases, she challenged these men in the name of their better books. Naturally, they had to meet the precocious writer who exuded such an air of authority.

How West became entangled with Wells is an often-told story, but Scott includes letters that provide the context for their ten-year affair and show how West eventually extricated herself by going to America in 1923. Scott includes a long letter that West sent to one of her sisters describing New York in the 1920s. It is of extraordinary interest as an almost documentary re-creation of a moment in history. The two biographies of West did not have the space to do this letter and others justice.

West crossed the Atlantic dozens of times in the 1920s and 1930s, writing stories, articles, and columns for *The New York Herald Tribune*, *The New York American*, *The Bookman*, *The New Republic*, and many other newspapers and journals. She warned of the rise of fascism and the likelihood of a second World War. She went to Washington and met many officials in the Roosevelt Administration, including Francis Biddle, who later became her lover during the Nuremberg trials. What makes West so indispensable is her acute literary and political sensibilities, her yoking of the psychological and the sociological, her understanding of the individual psyche and of bureaucracy. Only in her letters do you learn that while she supported the New Deal from the start, she had misgivings about its shoddy administration, poorly conceived programs, and lax security procedures. West never minced words and never pretended not to have visceral reactions to people which influenced her opinions of them: "Eleanor Roosevelt is the most hideous being imaginable and was dressed fantastically badly and radiated charm and vitality, partly the result of her lovely voice," West wrote to *New Yorker* editor Harold Ross, who commissioned many of her brilliant postwar reports on spy trials.

West's comment on Roosevelt demonstrates her penchant for exaggeration (most hideous? really?). For the most part, editor Scott lets West have her way with words, however extravagant, but occasionally in the notes the editor rightly feels compelled to point out errors in West's reports, or inaccurate gossip, or simply prejudices that other observers of the scene or members of her family did not share. Indeed, West sometimes wrote such fantastic letters that her reliability as a reporter—perhaps even her mental equilibrium—have to be questioned.

Such is the case with her account of Huey Long, which she sent to historian Arthur Schlesinger, Jr. I very much wanted to put this report in my biography of West, but I saw no way to verify her account or to integrate it into a narrative of her life. Now the letter is available and worth close study, both for what it says about Long and what it says about West. The letter weaves a most baroque tale that involves Long questioning her closely about an operation on her breasts. That she had such an operation I can verify, that Long knew about it without West telling him (as she asserts) seems very strange—or perhaps it sheds a whole new light on the Senator and Washington politics. I cannot make up my mind which.

The Long letter should be read in tandem with West's report of a UFO. She presents a most detailed account of a mysterious object in the sky which she tracked for a considerable period. She was not persuaded by the matter of fact explanation she received from her government. As in her investigation of spies and traitors, she knew when something was afoot—even if, in this case, she could not solve the mystery.

Although some of West's letters may strike one as the monologues of an ego-maniac and mythomane (to use the term West applied to those she thought had mythologized their lives) most of her correspondence is very sociable and engaging. She wants to tell her correspondents about herself, but she is eager to hear about their lives in return. Letters constituted a conversation for her.

Undoubtedly, there are some good letters left out of this volume. Another editor would surely have made some different selections. But Scott has chosen a representative collection, featuring the best letters on the subjects to which West kept returning. No reader needs, for example, every letter she wrote about her fraught relationship with her son, Anthony West. On the topic of family West often repeats herself—as most of us do. Nevertheless, there will be a need one day for a new selection, or an updating of Scott's volume, since many of West's letters remain in private hands, and others may still turn up that are thought to have been lost.

Because of her seventy-year literary career, West seemed to know or to observe everyone of importance in her century. She provides a smorgasbord of commentary on, variously, the Duke and Duchess of Windsor, Arnold Bennett (she called him one of her literary "uncles"), Lord Beaverbrook (one of her lovers), Janet Flanner (a *New Yorker* colleague), Emma Goldman, John Gunther (another lover), Violet Hunt, Fannie Hurst, D. H. Lawrence (one of her literary heroes), Sinclair Lewis, Senator Joseph McCarthy, Harold Macmillan (whose family published her), Somerset Maugham, Henry Miller, Sir Harold Nicolson, Anais Nin, Paul Robeson (there were friends in the 1920s), Harold Ross, Arthur Schlesinger (she thought him soft on Communism but they later became friends), May Sinclair, Dorothy Thompson, Tito, H.G. Wells, Oscar Wilde, Virginia Woolf, and Alexander Woollcott.

West's range of friends was astonishing—from British comic Frankie Howerd to CIA Director Allen Dulles. Her range of subjects was equally broad. She could elaborate the most Byzantine theories of history, then turn immediately to delicious gossip and anecdotes. Her letters are serious, flirtatious, and extremely funny. As one of her friends once said to me, "she gave good value." She had the gift of making anyone she spoke to—or wrote to—feel important.

It is sad to report that most of West's novels are out of print and that much else of her work has never been collected. In the last stages of her career she wrote brilliant book reviews for the London *Sunday Telegraph*. Indeed, Hilton Kramer called them at the time the best of their kind, and his assessment holds true. A selection of her hundreds of essays and book reviews deserves to be printed in two or three volumes. Perhaps this edition of the letters will spark the renewed interest needed to make Rebecca West our contemporary once more.

REBECCA WEST:
A PORTRAIT

I wanted to include this portrait as the preface to my biography of West, but my British publisher thought it just repeated what the rest of the biography had to show. In retrospect, I regret the decision to omit this lively piece, sacrificed, I suspect, because the page count of the biography was already more than what the publisher had bargained for. I published it in a literary journal, Confrontation, edited then by Martin Tucker, who heard me deliver the piece as a talk at the National Arts Club.

I spent over four years researching and writing the life of Rebecca West. My work included nine trips to Tulsa, Oklahoma to examine her massive archive, and nine trips to London and to other parts of England to interview her friends, family, and associates. Even when I traveled to Tulsa, I felt I was outside of my American born realm, immersing myself in a British world that I had not only to study but somehow to bring to life in a biography. It helped me to visit Chester Williams, who painted her portrait and who graciously invited me to stay with him and his charming wife to reminisce about my lively, formidable subject. I never tried to be anything other than an American to my generous and genial British hosts, who, like Rebecca West, were very fond of Americans. My subject seduced me, so that I began using her turns of phrase—calling raincoats mackintoshes—and indulging in habits of speech I preserved in the American edition of my biography, even though at least one reviewer resented it. I regard the portrait I have written, which is derived primarily from my interviews, as similar to a collection of outtakes—those precious bits of film that do not make the final cut but which tell much about the film and its making. Implicit in my portrait, in other words, is a record of the elsewhere I had to go to do my biography.

If you are reading the biography of virtually any significant British or American writer—from say 1910 to 1980—you may find a reference to Rebecca West. The biographer will probably be quoting from one of her book reviews or reminiscences, for she was among the finest critics and raconteurs of her age, and indeed of any age. Virginia Woolf once wrote to her "as an admirer who actually drove 8 miles the other day to buy a copy of the Daily Telegraph in order not to miss your article. This is not an effort I am in the habit of making, but a proof of the great admiration with which I hold your work."

Because Rebecca could speak as brilliantly as she wrote, her words made the rounds in the Anglo-American literary community—a much more cohesive world than can be imagined in the midst of today's culture of multi-national conglomerates. England and America served as her platform in a way not available to literary figures today. Via television, a writer reaches more people than she did, but not with the alternately seductive and astringent prose of a brilliant mind at the top of her form as a journalist and biographer, possessed of a flamboyant imagination that made her a formidable novelist as well. The entry on her in the *Columbia Encyclopedia* contains the succinct verdict: "one of the finest writers of prose in 20th century Britain."

Rebecca in person provoked startled comments. Virginia Woolf has left the most vivid portrait: "a cross between a charwoman and a gipsy, but as tenacious as a terrier, with flashing eyes." Virginia found Rebecca an unkempt genius and called her a "hardened liar," but she also admired her "immense vitality" and intelligence. Virginia liked Rebecca even as she picked out her flaws. Rebecca reciprocated, lauding Virginia's uncompromising feminism and Leonardo beauty, but faulting her for untidiness, saying she was not "turned out well" and looked as though she had been "drawn through a hedge backwards." Rebecca had an engaging directness that threatened yet exhilarated Virginia: "Rebecca was fascinating—ungainly, awkward, powerful, arborial, like some sloth or mandrill; but oh what a joy to grapple with her hairy arms! I mean she was very upstanding and outspoken, and we discussed religion, sex, literature, and other problems…for 3 hours." A dismayed Rebecca lived to read Virginia's letters and objected that she did not have hairy arms!

It is difficult to believe that anyone could be better company than Rebecca West. That was H.G. Wells's verdict, who could be the best of company himself. Always a performer, she loved entertaining friends and meeting new people. She loved listening to the latest gossip, if she was not, indeed, inventing it herself, putting her indelible mark on what she had just heard. She once asked writer Jilly Cooper about a mutual friend. How was he getting on with his "host of black lovers?" When Jilly observed that he'd had the same lover for years, Rebecca, with several pairs of spectacles dangling from her neck, replied "Oh well, it must be my spectacles seeing quadruple."

Rebecca flashed through places and lives and left behind a fearful vacuum. Her "darting, dragon-fly" dialogue" could leave her company gasping in her wake, and wondering "what did she mean about…If only I had asked her about…" Coming into a party she halted and in a loud stage whisper observed, "My first solicitor, a bad choice."

The journalist Dorothy Thompson, one of Rebecca's fondest friends, said: "you always invite a conversation." Rebecca wanted to give good value. Receiving a gift meant putting the ball into play, hoping her correspondent or conversationalist would bat it back, continuing the game. Thanking her niece, Alison Macleod, for a Christmas present of chocolate covered plums for Rebecca's husband, Rebecca remarked: "Henry is mad on prunes in any form and I feed them to him on a conveyor-belt." Rebecca talked about everything. She loved "nice ladies' clothing conversations." She greeted one American visitor with an allusion to the television soap, *Dallas*: "And who do *you* think shot Mr. J.R.?"

Several friends attested to her ability to draw them out. She did not impose herself on her company. "She *made* me loquacious. She made me articulate," remembers magazine editor, Fleur Cowles, who often invited Rebecca to her Sussex home. "She made you feel like you were the person she really wanted to meet," actor Michael Denison observes. During a party at her country home Rebecca spotted Rosalind Burdon-Taylor, the daughter of Greta Mortimer, an old acting school chum, "There you are. I've just named a cow after you!" Rebecca was just as kind to her hairdresser, Joan White, wanting to know how she was doing and whether Joan was really all right. When Rebecca read about a raid on a brothel in Streatham, where Joan lived, Rebecca greeted her: "And what have *you* been up to?"

Rebecca loved the act of naming and peopled her world with many different versions of herself. Writing to her sisters, she often signed herself Anne, an allusion to her role as precocious baby sister who insisted that her mispronunciation of antelope (antelopy) was correct. Of course she was Panther to H.G. Wells and to a select circle of friends. In married life she was Rac to Henry's Ric, (names of dogs in a French cartoon). She liked to style herself Auntie to her nieces and nephews and cousins. Depending on her mood and company, she might be Aunt Cicily (or Cissie), Aunt Rebecca, Dame Cicily, Dame Rebecca, or even Becky. To Margaret Hodges (one of Rebecca's secretaries and a lifelong friend), Rebecca styled herself Simpkin, cozy and cross and always getting herself into the craziest scrapes:

On Saturday evening it became evident Lady Kelly had forgotten that she had invited the Director of Personnel in the Foreign Office and his wife for Saturday dinner & Sunday lunch. Thus it happened that they were told to use what had been my bathroom. Which had (I do not know why) no lock on the door. Hence I now know what a Director of Personnel in the Foreign Office looks like without a stitch on. Knowledge of this sort is rarely acquired by octogenarians.

Rebecca once suggested that Joan White call her "Auntie Rebecca." Joan said "No thank you." She felt more comfortable with Dame Rebecca, and before that, Mrs. Andrews. Joan had done Rebecca's hair for nearly fifty years, but she was not about to play her employer's shifting games of identity. After a gall bladder operation, while still under the sway of an anesthetic, a delirious Rebecca envisioned her three names clashing in her head: "Cicily Fairfield, Cicily Andrews, Rebecca West, I could not choose between them."

Rebecca West's force as a writer and a personality derived from her power to make profound connections between seemingly disparate subjects. "Opera in Greenville," the title of her incomparable article on a lynching trial, suggests how she made an art out of reporting and found in public events the metaphors of great literature. This talent for making life congruent led also to paranoia and conspiracy theories; her quick and restless mind craved solutions. Late at night, in her old age, she worked algebra equations; it soothed her to find answers, to submit herself to a discipline with exact outcomes.

Rebecca's penchant for fetching her proofs from afar could be whimsical and fantastic. Genealogy became an especially useful aid. Watching the American film of *Carmen Jones*, she detected a resemblance between herself and the black singer Pearl Bailey. Not so surprising, Rebecca claimed, because a remote and roving Highland ancestor had returned home with an African bride, and this Berber, a woman of musical gifts, had brought one of her instruments. Alas, Rebecca's nearer ancestors, ashamed of their African relation, had destroyed the evidence for this claim. (How Rebecca knew it to be true without the evidence did not trouble her.) This trace of Berber blood (Rebecca was dark complected as a child) encouraged her to hope she might have a familial connection with her favorite church father, the North African Bishop, St. Augustine, whose biography she wrote with her accustomed flair for finding intimate and psychologically revealing details. No writer but Rebecca West could begin an anecdote with Pearl Bailey and end with Saint Augustine.

Life was an astounding drama. "I have just had the most incredible experience," she would write a friend. "Really, things are very odd," she would inform another. Or, she would ring up to announce: "The most unfortunate thing has just happened," and elaborate a baroque tale of mishaps. A family member would get a clarion call: "LOOK HERE. THIS IS REBECCA." Part of the clamor in her later years can be attributed to increasing deafness and failing eyesight which could make her edgy and irritable. But just as often she would negotiate these disabilities with courage and aplomb. She hated calling attention to her infirmity, and she was caught, more than once, crawling up stairs rather than admit she could no longer climb them on her feet. She almost never stopped writing, no matter how difficult her health and personal circumstances might become. Even those who worked with her for many years, however, could not be certain of her moods. She might react to a remark by roaring "WHAT?"—or the truly terrifying "WHAT? WHAT?" And you could not be sure if she had not heard you or had decided you had just uttered a particularly noxious bit of nonsense.

She was terribly kind to friends, supporting them with money if necessary, and taking careful note of their troubles in her diaries, especially those written in her last years. The family conflicts of her friends she took to heart, knowing all too well what her own painful clashes with her family had cost her. Again and again it was the family to which she returned, brooding about her own in countless letters and in diaries, making it the focus of both her fiction and nonfiction.

She was not fair with people—if what is meant by that term is an even-handed, dispassionate appraisal of character. One of her letters begins: "Just a few moments of abandonment to the pleasures of defamation." She enjoyed building cases against people, assembling briefs that would be the envy of any attorney. Indeed, she would have made a great lawyer. She enjoyed employing legions of them, and writing minute accounts of parties who had traduced her, meanwhile getting in her innings against them. She felt bereft without a good lawyer in hand, as she told one of her favorites: "I cannot tell you how often I have thought of you with the wistfulness which might have been expected from someone thinking of a lost love—but believe me the emotions excited by the thought of a lost solicitor can be quite as poignant."

Rebecca was often tolerant and understanding of those she found sympathetic. although even fond friends might feel the lash—like an Australian confidant she described as that "monstrous misbirth of the Southern Hemisphere." As for others, well they were often dispatched in a phrase—a "goose down to the last feather," Rebecca said of a certain Bloomsbury lady (Frances Partridge). Novelist Michael Arlen, once Rebecca's confidant and then banished, became: "every other inch a gentleman." Charles Curran, her beloved friend and colleague at

London's *Evening Standard*, once told her that she had the reputation of a "hell-cat with a tongue made of broken bottles and dipped in acid."

Rebecca was intimidating. She thought her name change from Cicily Fairfield to Rebecca West—taken from Ibsen's feisty heroine—contributed to her formidable reputation for leveling people with her tongue. In some moods, she regretted the pseudonym. But as one of her friends remarked, "If she'd changed her name to Thistledown Dewdrop she *still* would have frightened people."

Her literary likes and dislikes were legendary. "I am dead to Dante. Beatrice is the great boring female of all time." She specialized in one-liners. To a query about Malcolm Muggeridge, she replied: "I can never think Christ is grateful for being alluded to as if He were a lost cause." She worshipped Proust and spent hours writing out her own translations of his work. D.H. Lawrence became a saint of modern literature in her "Elegy." Joyce got full marks for genius and a rap for bad taste. Dostoevsky inspired her Russian novel, *The Birds Fall Down*. She thought Tolstoy the "most bogus great writer of all time." *War and Peace* was full of stock characters rendered conventionally, and the whole thing broke down in a wrangle about an absurd theory of history. Yet he had only to say that "when he was a child he went to a dancing-class and saw a little girl with ringlets who danced clumsily for everybody to break into sobs and cry, 'What marvellous powers of observation.'"

She despised Henry Miller, the man and his work. She first met him in Paris in Anais Nin's apartment. Rebecca happened to be passing the bathroom and heard a gurgling sound. She opened the door and there was Henry Miller committing suicide by drowning himself in the bathtub. "So I pulled the plug and walked out," Rebecca confided to a friend. "You know, he never thanked me." At the first night party for *Death of a Salesman* in London a man asked Rebecca what she thought of the play. "Twaddle! What was he [Willie Loman] going on about? Judging by the backdrop he owned one of the most valuable bits of real estate in Manhattan." She did not know that her opinion had been solicited by the play's author, Arthur Miller.

"[A] mercenary young scoundrel who is a member of the Communist Party," she called Norman Mailer. "I think he probably wrote 'The Naked and the Dead' under instruction as one of a programme of work designed to discredit the American army and navy." He had no literary merit whatsoever. His novel, *The Deer Park*, was a piece of pornography she would have to be paid to finish reading. "A dreary bore, to meet or to read," he had "as much brain as a road drill." Even though his brand of the nonfiction novel owes much to her example in *Black*

Lamb and Grey Falcon and *The Meaning of Treason*, she pronounced him "a peacock without any tail."

Rebecca scorned Margaret Drabble. All those domestic scenes in her novels of washing up, all that harping on housework! Even worse, Drabble had done an admiring biography of Rebecca's *bete noire*, Arnold Bennett. Antonia Fraser, on the other hand, was a favorite. When her biography of Mary, Queen of Scots, became a best seller, Rebecca exclaimed: "All that lovely money you're getting! You grab it, you spend it, you enjoy it. Don't save it. Don't feel guilty about it. You're young and pretty, enjoy it." That was not the reaction Antonia was getting from others.

Rebecca had no time for her countryman, Sir Walter Scott. When he did not bore her and make her yawn, he was forcing the pace of his novels, filling them full of bluster and brawling. Even his heroines languished with an "open throttle." She once visited his great home, Abbottsford, with her nephew Norman Macleod and his family. The guide explained in suitably reverential tones that during his dying days Sir Walter preferred the dining room with its marvelous view of the Tweed. There one morning at 11:00 a.m. he expired. Rebecca continued the story: "Then everybody said "good we can have lunch.'"

She spent a lifetime denigrating T.S. Eliot, detesting his phony erudition and its baleful influence on literary criticism. She could not abide hearing him defended. During one argument with the editor of the *Times Literary Supplement*, she brought herself to the peak of vehemence when he suggested she might allow that Eliot got full marks for his sensitivity. "Eliot? Sensitivity? As much sensitivity as Marks & Spencer!"

Among the new generation of feminist writers in the 1970s, Rebecca preferred Kate Millet, finding Germaine Greer's *The Female Eunuch* a puzzle: "She approves of sex but never in the way that anybody else does it…. If the gentleman takes any steps to make the proceedings interesting, he is regarding her as a sex object. If the lady tries to make the proceedings pleasurable, then she is abasing herself and castrating herself. I cannot think what form there is left for sexual relations to take, except a sort of fire-drill."

Friends were warmly received and made to feel she valued their company. "Now when are you coming to see me again," she might say as a visitor disengaged from her embrace—it would, like as not, be a good hug. If too much time had elapsed between meetings, she would send a note pointing out that the interval had been too long. As the late Leo Lerman said, a friendship with Rebecca always had in it the suggestion of a love affair. When she stayed with Noel Coward at his home in France, there was always raucous laughter and flirtation. When

Noel's secretary, Cole Lesley, bid her good night saying, "You know where my room is don't you, if you want anything in the night." "Coley," she said, "I've received many invitations in my life: *never* so direct a one as that. But must you put all the initiative on me?" She did appear in his room at a quarter to five in the morning, but alas what drove her to it was a gall bladder attack.

Late at night, after dinner, the theater, and a party, Rebecca was escorted back to her Kensington flat. Now in her late seventies she had trouble undoing her dress and asked Tom Guinzberg, the son of her American publisher Harold Guinzberg, the founder of The Viking Press, to help her unzip. "It would be a pleasure," he offered "I think you mean it would be a privilege, dear Tom," she replied.

A regular Rebecca West correspondent would receive several letters a year and learn about the state of her health—something was always wrong with her teeth, her eyes, her digestive system (that old perennial gastro-enteritis)—her family (the saga of her son Anthony) strange visitors who delighted or plagued her. She wanted a record—"in case I join the heavenly choir or some other pop group soon." The stories went on and on, and many of them were rattling good fun; others were a morose screed of misfortune—dark, dark, dark tales that, she thought, suggested a supernatural hex against her. There would be reminiscences of H.G. (as she always called him), T.E. Lawrence, Charlie Chaplin, and many other greats as well as fetching descriptions of her travels and her country house.

She had the timing of a great comedian. On William F. Buckley's Firing Line television program, in the midst of making a point about the intelligence services—that they should come clean and confess they could not keep secrets very well and also reveal "who shot whom"—Buckley interrupted to say "What do you mean, 'who shot whom.'" She paused and then brought down the house with two words expressed in a hushed voice: "What innocence!"

Not everyone was charmed. "She bored me a good deal on the few occasions when we met," Kingsley Amis wrote to me. "She bristled and barked staccato orders at me," Kenneth Tynan claimed, "and threw gauntlets in all directions. How can a woman contrive to be a non-smoker and yet look all the time as if she were chewing a cheroot." Rebecca reciprocated with the comment that Tynan had the "curious appearance of being a neatly-dressed corpse."

Reality often took Rebecca by storm; it overcame her and she spoke like a Cassandra. She wrote a letter to Arthur Crook, editor of *The Times Literary Supplement*, saying that reviewers treated her like a witch casting maleficent spells. She was something of a prophetess—about public and private life, matters great and small. She once dreamed that her bedroom wall had given way to a scene in which policeman were marking the ground with tape. She asked one of them what had happened. He said. "It was a flat." What? she asked. "A flat, a flat, a flat," he impatiently cried. She would read about it in the newspapers the next day, he told her. The morrow brought news of Donald Maclachlan's death, the *Sunday Telegraph* editor who had invited her to be the paper's reviewer. Rebecca called friends, trying to find out exactly how he died. On the phone she was told that he had had an accident on the road. She had trouble hearing the explanation, and her friend shouted, "It was a flat, a flat, a flat."

Rebecca West had the great honor and misfortune to declare Communism a dud. Never for a moment did she consider the 1917 revolution the wave of the future. To this day, significant elements of the Left have never forgiven her for being right. Her position cost her friends and earned her enmity. It was damned indecent of her not to have had at least some initial enthusiasm for the great experiment.

Her politics were intricate, and you do them no justice by trying to align her on the Left or the Right. As she said of Thackeray, she was "striped like the zebra with radicalism and conservatism." An anonymous writer in *Time and Tide* said it best: "It is probable that if there is ever an English Revolution there will come a point when the Reds and Whites will sink their differences for ten minutes while they guillotine Miss West for making remarks that both sides have found intolerably unhelpful."

Although she was a modern and progressive thinker in many respects, that same *Time and Tide* writer astutely linked her with an earlier age: "It is quite easy to imagine her a contemporary of Lady Mary Wortley Montague. Gossiping yet keenly analytic, rambling and yet sharply satirical, frank to the point of coarseness yet in love with elegance, her work has the very character of eighteenth-century writing." No writer has provided better talk since Samuel Johnson. Had she been served by her own Boswell her wit would be seen to rival his. One of her editors has said as much. That she has not become as celebrated as Samuel would not surprise her: "Men are more given to eccentricity than women: a female Doctor Johnson would not be remembered favourably."

H.G. Wells said there would never be another like her. He was speaking of the person. Frank Swinnerton said there would never be another like her. He was speaking of the critic. She was enormous fun. People adored her. She was dangerous. She scared people. Both her humor and her anger were explosive. As her niece Alison has said, if she were to return, it would have to be as a firework.

THE BIOGRAPHER WHO CAME IN FROM THE COLD: BECOMING REBECCA WEST'S AUTHORIZED BIOGRAPHER

I wrote this long piece for Biography and Source Studies. Rebecca West wrote a good deal about biography, contributed to many biographies of her contemporaries, and, of course, wrote biography herself. She had an ambivalent attitude toward the genre, an uneasiness that I explore in this essay. This essay also allows me (the biographer) to talk about myself, thereby providing, I hope, some insight into how I shaped the life of my subject.

> This is your last job...Then you can come in from the cold."—Control to Alec Leamas, *The Spy Who Came in From the Cold*

We all compose novels of our own lives. The plot I have chosen for myself most closely resembles that of a John Le Carré novel. I used to be taken with the idea of the biographer as a detective. But then what is the crime the biographer/detective is investigating? And who is the criminal? In contemporary fiction, the criminal is usually the biographer. He is the spy in William Golding's novel, *The Paper Men*, caught by his subject in the act of rifling through his subject's garbage.

My spying began in 1980 with the research I did for a biography of Marilyn Monroe. Although working on this book remained a pleasure, two episodes proved to be deeply disturbing. When I called Whitey Snyder, Marilyn's favorite makeup man and confidant, he treated me with scarcely veiled hostility. He had spoken to too many biographers already, he said. I tried my usual ploy: I was an academic especially interested in her work as an actress, an approach to Monroe that biographers had not handled very well. I tried asking a few innocuous questions just to get him warmed up. I tried mentioning names of people I had already interviewed and who I knew he respected. I tried and tried in an agonizing phone call that lasted perhaps five minutes—with me doing most of the talking—and then I gave up and said goodbye.

There is nothing very remarkable about this rejection in itself, except that most biographers do not dwell on their rebuffs. Although they may feel rather aggrieved that someone has decided not to cooperate with them, biographers cannot afford to be too introspective—especially while working on a biography. To brood over the nature of biography as a rude and transgressive genre would probably result in abandonment of the project. Biographers are intruders—that was the message Whitey conveyed to me. And I do not believe I have made a single phone call to an interviewee since my call to him without a considerable degree of reluctance. I have been told off a few times or made to feel like an interloper. Indeed, many biographies have never seen the light of day precisely because the biographer cannot stomach the opposition that arises as soon as he or she begins asking impertinent questions.

I know biographers who have avoided this troubling aspect of biography by dealing with figures who are long dead and do not have surviving friends or family who might be interviewed. But that is really a dodge. You can be sure that Leon Edel and Richard Ellmann would not have had the blessings of Henry James and James Joyce. The latter novelist called my colleagues "biografiends," and the former not only burnt his letters to foil future biographers, he wrote two works of fiction that expose biographers as a breed of skulking spies.

In *The Aspern Papers*, the better known of James's two broadsides against biography, an erstwhile biographer of Jeffrey Aspern, an early nineteenth-century poet, visits Venice hoping to acquire the correspondence between Aspern and his mistress, Miss Bordereau. Insinuating himself into Miss Bordereau's life, the biographer takes her niece, Tita, into his confidence. After Miss Bordereau catches him searching through her desk, he leaves for a few days. When he returns after a fortnight, he finds that she has died. Tita has fallen in love with him and intimates that only a relative can be permitted to examine the papers. Alarmed at this proposal, the biographer leaves, only to find at his next meeting with Tita that she has destroyed the letters. This is the story in which James coins a memorable term for the biographer: a "publishing scoundrel."

In "The Real Right Thing," George Withermore, an inexperienced young journalist and critic, is flattered by an invitation from the widow of the great writer Ashton Doyne to write her recently deceased husband's biography—especially since she gives him complete access to Doyne's papers and puts him to work in the writer's study. Withermore immerses himself in Doyne's archive, and at first is encouraged by the almost palpable presence of his subject, and then he begins to have second thoughts.

James wrote the latter tale while embarking on a biography of the American poet and sculptor, William Wetmore Story. As Leon Edel suggests in his biography of James, the novelist seems to have wondered whether he was doing the right thing in abandoning fiction for biography. "The Real Right Thing" reads like a Gothic ghost story, with the biographer portrayed as a kind of grave robber, awakening the spirit of the deceased. James, of course, did not invent this attitude toward biography: "Biography is one of the new terrors of death," wrote John Arbuthnot (1667-1735). But James blackens the biographical quest as if to shrive himself. In fact, "The Real Right Thing" is cloaked in black. Doyne's widow greets the biographer in her "large array of mourning—with big black eyes, her big black wig, her big black fan and gloves…." She encourages the biographer to work in the evenings "for quiet and privacy." But those evening sessions reveal that the biographer is working in the dark. It is on such a "black London November" that Withermore begins to doubt he has the right to plumb Doyne's life: "What warrant had he ever received from Ashton Doyne himself for so direct and, as it were, so familiar an approach?" Yet for nearly a month the biographer labors to believe in the "consecration of his enterprise." Words like warrant and consecration suggest just how badly biographers want to believe that they are blessed. This self-delusion is what leads Stephen Oates, for example, to announce in his biography of Faulkner that his subject appeared to him in a dream to sanction Oates's enterprise. I cannot think of anything more unlikely than Faulkner, a writer with a great Gothic imagination and a detestation of prying biographers, spending a moment in his afterlife to anoint Oates. It is far more likely that Oates, like Withermore, misread the meaning of his subject's appearance. In this case, Oates apparently failed to spot the horsewhip in Faulkner's hand.

Biographers are moles, trespassers, and burglars—as James dramatizes by having Withermore "dipping, deep into some of Doyne's secrets." The biographer delights in "drawing curtains, forcing many doors, reading many riddles, going, in general, as they said, behind almost everything." Biographers go for the back story, the hidden side of the subject's face, as Edel himself acknowledged with relish when he changed a Jamesian term, "the figure in the carpet," to describe the biographer's quest to find the "figure under the carpet." That banal cliché about sweeping things under the carpet becomes a Gothic horror in the biographer's mission. So deluded is Withermore at one point that he imagines Doyne's presence as a kind of breath of the holy spirit lingering over the "young priest at his altar." It does not occur to the biographer, so dedicated to resurrecting a life, that to others he is creating a kind of Frankenstein, a semblance of a human being, but certainly not "the real right thing." His enterprise is not right morally and not right aesthetically.

It is precisely at the moment of his exaltation that Withermore senses Doyne's withdrawal from him. The biographer's "protected state"—largely a figment of his imagination—disintegrates, and doubts about his business begin to gather. Now the biographer experiences the "monstrous oppression" of his subject, "who becomes a burden the biographer cannot tolerate. Suddenly the widow appears as "the tall black lady." Withermore no longer feels in league with her but rather on the other side, so to speak—that is, on the side of his subject, who is signaling through Withermore's uneasiness Doyne's wish that the biography should proceed no further. "I feel I'm wrong," the biographer tells the widow. Rather than giving his subject a new life, Withermore contends that in writing about Doyne, "We lay him bare. We serve him up. What is it called? We give him to the world." Exposing his "original simplicity" as a misunderstanding, the biographer concludes, "But I understand at last. He only wanted to communicate. He strains forward out of his darkness; he reaches toward us out of his mystery; he makes us dim signs out of his horror." The uncomprehending widow replies "Horror?" Withermore explains: "At what we're doing.... He's there to *save* his life. He's there to be let alone." The widow, thinking only of the precious biography, "almost shrieked": "So you give up." Like a character in a Gothic tale, she exclaims: "You *are* afraid!" And indeed, the biographer is terrified, telling her that Doyne is "there as a curse!" And the curse carries moral and spiritual weight: "I *should* give up!" Withermore emphasizes.

The widow has seen the biography as a gift to her husband, a tribute to his importance. But then the biographer essays one more attempt to climb the stairs to his subject's study, only to return to say Doyne is on the threshold "guarding it." So Withermore did not enter? she asks. "He forbids!" Withermore says in such a commanding voice that after an instant the widow concedes "Give up." Then she decides to mount the stairs herself but returns, acknowledging that her dead husband still blocks the way. "I give up," are her last words.

By and large, biographers who do not give up do not wish to confront the harrowing aspects of biography. I have heard biographers joke about their work in archives, saying they like to read other peoples's mail. I think they find it comforting that those documents are housed in a public repository, as if such institutions sanction their research. Even better if the biographer gets a grant, another sign of approval. But the truth is biography remains invasive, however you dress it up. As Leamas says to his East German interrogator, "We're all the same, you know, that's the joke."

But there is another side to the problems of prying biographers—which leads me to the second episode that disturbed my equilibrium while exploring the life of Marilyn Monroe. After a few years of working on the biography, I had formed a tight circle of friends/interviewees who had come to believe in my book and who wanted to do everything in their power to assist me. Two of these people—I shall have to call them X and Y—gave me a sense not of the movie star and the actress but of the day-to-day woman. In late 1984, toward the end of a conversation with X, she began to discuss Marilyn's last days. She lowered her voice: "You know Y was very good to Marilyn and always wanted to help. Unfortunately, that help sometimes took the form of drugs." To this day, I have not seen this aspect of Monroe's biography addressed, for most of the talk of her taking uppers and downers involves her doctors.

I could see no way then to tell what I knew without divulging the identities of X and Y, who were already present in the biography but not directly implicated in the story of how she died. And I still have to resort to calling the principals X and Y because they are alive, and I would be betraying the confidence of X if I said any more—not to mention destroying the friendship between X and Y.

But what is the point of writing biography if you cannot tell the secrets you learn? I felt not only deeply frustrated, since I wanted to enrich an appreciation of the circumstances in which Monroe died, I also felt like a spy who was expected to hold back information in order to present a cover story, so to speak. That this remained the only story I had to hold back for this biography did not make me feel any better, and my suppression of part of the story continues to rankle. I decided then never to submit to such a self-imposed gag order again. Or so I thought.

In both episodes with Whitey Snyder and X and Y, I had to confront the unseemly side of biography that most biographers—like good spies—do their best to conceal. Have you ever noticed how over-the-top the acknowledgments sections of biographies tend to be? The biographer does not just thank everyone (and the list can go on for pages and pages) for their generous help, those acknowledgees are made to seem heroic, kind, thoughtful—you name it—paragons of virtue. (For a state of the art example of what I mean, read the Acknowledgments in Blake Bailey's biography of Richard Yates.) I suppose biographers should not be blamed for this sort of flattery. It is right to thank people, of course, and who knows when some of those folks will come in handy again? Laying it on thick is one of the ways a biographer builds up a network of contacts that might become useful for the next book. (Researching Marilyn Monroe provided me with invaluable Hollywood sources I called on while working on my biography of Lillian Hellman.) But if you are a biographer, you know that some of those people the biographer so fulsomely thanks cannot possibly be *that good.* In our contemporary language, we'd have to say those acknowledgments just do not compute. I have to hand it to Jerry Oppenheimer, biographer of Martha Stewart, for using his Acknowledgments in a novel way to thank some of his interviewees: all of the people "Martha stepped on along the way." Jerry might be mean-spirited, but he is also therapeutic. Debunking biographies often release the passions other biographers may feel but dare not express in their books. In his vastly overrated recent biography of John Kennedy, Robert Dallek, for example, is quite happy to exploit Seymour Hersh's revelations about Kennedy's sex life in *The Dark Side of Camelot* while writing an introduction that sanctimoniously refers to his "balanced" view of his subject and the need to rise above all the debunking biographies. Without Sy the Spy, a superb interviewer who ferrets out the nitty-gritty, Dallek's soporific book would lose what little steam it has.

Reading acknowledgments, when you have done the job yourself, becomes an exercise in decoding. The biographer, like a good spy, simply cannot reveal how he got all those people to talk. Some are willing witnesses, of course, but all of them? It just all fell into place because the biographer is such a good guy, a stand-up woman? Dallek does not even refer to interviews—just to talks and conversations. How deceptively comfortable it makes biography seem. No one had to be coaxed, flattered, or pressured? What the acknowledgments do not tell us is how the biographer manipulates his sources and vice versa. Janet Malcolm is one of the few writers to be candid about this jockeying for position between interviewer and interviewee. In *The Silent Woman*, she makes us privy to what she is thinking as she talks to the principals in Sylvia Plath's life, and what she is thinking is, "How can I get the information I want?"

In *The Blood Doctor*, Barbara Vine (Ruth Rendell), provides a rare insight into the biographer at work. Martin Nanther cajoles, bites his tongue, and does whatever the situation requires to keep his interviewees talking. "I nod sympathetically," he notes—not because he is sympathetic to what is said but simply to further the conversation, to establish a rapport with the interviewee. Meanwhile Martin withholds what he is really thinking and does not contradict the witness when she is mis-stating or even lying about the facts. Sometimes Martin lies to protect the information he already has. One interviewee asks him not to mention a certain party to another and Martin agrees, already knowing that he will break his promise because it is the only way to elicit the information he seeks. In another case, he violates an agreement that his interviewee thought was implicit in their conversation, and Martin comments: "I remind him that when he asked for an undertaking I didn't answer him."

Martin's behavior is not surprising to me. When I decided to write my biography of Martha Gellhorn in the spring of 1988, I wrote to her asking for an interview. She wrote a polite letter declining the honor. I decided to go ahead because I did not believe I needed her approval, and because I felt there was still a slight possibility that she might relent and provide at least limited cooperation. I then made a strategic Martin Nauther-like decision. I flew to St. Louis to interview every one of her childhood friends and schoolmates I could find, as well as friends of her parents. Some of these witnesses were still in touch with Martha; many had not heard from her in decades. Only a few asked me if I had her cooperation. To them, I simply said that I hoped to get it. I did not go into any detail, and to my relief they asked no more questions.

The trip to St. Louis became exhilarating as I gathered new material from interviews with people in their eighties who might not be available for biographers awaiting Martha's death. It is curious, by the way, that it is the unauthorized biographer of the living figure who becomes an object of hate. Those biographers who lie in wait, or conduct deathwatches, anticipating that moment when their subject is no more so that the biography can proceed apace, are, strangely, regarded as the responsible types. Agnes DeMille waited decades for Martha Graham to die so that she could publish the biography of her friend. It had been all ready to go the moment Graham departed this world. "That was rather sneaky of me, wasn't it?" DeMille said to her biographer Carol Easton. Am I alone in thinking there is something ghoulish about Scott Berg's grave-robbing memoir/biography, published less than two weeks after Katharine Hepburn's death? Well, there are those of us who spy on the living and those of us who dig up the dead.

In countless interviews, Berg presents a picture of biographer and subject that is positively homey. But I have never made a trip like the one to St. Louis without feeling at some point a profound deracination. It usually occurs at night in a hotel room when I realize I am all alone, *adrift*—that the only one really supporting this adventure is me. A fellow biographer once confessed to me that she also had such moments, and they made her feel suicidal. The unauthorized biography is, among other things, a tremendous act of will. At such Alec Leamas moments, I vow that this will be my last job and now I can come in from the cold. Like

Alec, I know that any moment I could be abandoned—as I was when Doubleday violated its own contract for the Gellhorn biography, caving in to the pressure my subject exerted to quash the book. My agent had to re-sell it to St. Martin's Press. One reason why I wanted my wife, Lisa Paddock, to co-author a biography of Susan Sontag with me was so that she could take on an even greater share of the burden than she had already assumed as my legal advisor on my other biographies (see "Susan Sontag: The Making of a Biography," in *Female Icons: Marilyn Monroe to Susan Sontag.*

Much of my life has been spent working on unauthorized biographies of subjects who have treated me with suspicion, contempt, and hostility. Arthur Miller, for example, did not answer my letters asking for an interview about Marilyn Monroe. In desperation, I attended a Hopwood Festival celebration at the University of Michigan, where Miller, once a student winner of a Hopwood for one of his earliest plays, was the featured speaker. He spent a portion of his talk reminiscing about his former wife. During a reception for him after his talk, I entered the circle around him and introduced myself, reminding him that I had written to him and that I wanted to ask him a few questions about Monroe. He stared at me and solemnly asked: "What is your question?" I began to stammer at the thought of ONE question, and as I began to formulate it, a woman, book in hand, barged in asking for his autograph. He smiled at her, took the book, and majestically turned his back on me. I suppose I could have tapped him on the shoulder and said, "Hold on, here's the question!" Instead, I slunk away.

After completing a draft of the biography, I sent it to Miller, saying only that I thought he should see it. I hoped, of course, that he would comment. I hoped that he would see my book was serious, see that I had treated him with respect and compassion. I hoped he would appreciate that I had avoided Mailer's rather mean spirited portrait, in which he remarks on Miller's parsimony by observing that no one could remember Miller ever picking up the check after a meal. I dreamed the playwright would grant an interview. I fantasized that he would blurb the biography. Miller did send a short reply, which said only that as with all manuscripts that came without a self-addressed envelope and postage, he had thrown my work into the wastebasket.

At best, I have been treated with benign neglect; at worst, with threats of lawsuits. The prevailing view of me has been as a spy. I say this without the slightest feeling of remorse or regret for my actions. Like Alec Leamas, I am case-hardened. I don't believe that the authorized biographer has any moral superiority over me; in some cases, quite the contrary. Authorized biography often strikes me as a put-up job. In two instances, I have become, in effect, an authorized biographer, although I did not seek the title and became so as the result of a chain reaction that I could not have foreseen.

I began as a spy, and I have remained a spy, although I was "turned"—to use the language of spies—and became a kind of double agent, which is how I think of authorized biographers. They have an inherent conflict of interest. On the one hand, they spy on their subjects, dipping into the secrets a la Withermore. On the other hand, they are spies for their subjects, searching out evidence that promotes their subjects. What else could authorized mean, whether you are a biographer or a Toyota dealer?

It all began in the spring of 1987 while I was at work on my second biography, *Lillian Hellman: Her Legend and Her Legacy* (1988). I read Lillian Hellman's review of *H. G. Wells and Rebecca West* by Gordon Ray. He had contrived a narrative around letters H. G. had sent to Rebecca between 1913 and 1923, the period that encompassed their intense and stormy love affair. H. G. destroyed Rebecca's correspondence, but she could not bear to obliterate his sexy, funny, and provoking prose, which he embellished with amusing illustrations. Ray's book is a little gem, marred only by Rebecca's heavy supervision—the price of gaining exclusive access to her archive at Yale. Hellman did not like this lop-sided aspect of the book, and she twitted West for allowing Ray to write about her lover's letters. Hellman's reservations amused me, since she had made a career of writing about her thirty-year on-and-off affair with Dashiell Hammett, and she had not been averse to revealing the intimacies of their relationship. Hellman's review also had a subtext: As a Stalinist she bitterly rejected West, a vehement anti-Communist. But more of that when I come to the early stages of how I became (most improbably) Rebecca West's authorized biographer.

Hellman's review kindled my interest in Rebecca West, for I could tell even from Hellman's jaundiced attitude that Rebecca had a wonderful life full of lovers, literary achievement, and fascinating political involvements. Sooner or later, I thought, I would make her my biographical subject. But I had to finish with Hellman, and the final phases of that biography inevitably led me to my biography of Martha Gellhorn (see "Martha and Me: The Promise and Peril of Unauthorized Biography," in *Biography and Source Studies* 7 [17-51]).

After Gellhorn, I wanted to do West, but there was a problem. Victoria Glendinning's well received, if brief, biography had been published in 1987, and West's Yale archive remained closed until the death of her son, who was still very much alive. Not willing, however, to abandon Rebecca, I proposed doing a book called "Counterfeit Lives," which would include chapters on the liaisons between Hammett and Hellman, Hemingway and Gellhorn, and West and Wells—plus a few other couples (the cast kept changing as I tinkered with seven different versions of a proposal my agent was never able to sell). The premise of the book had to do with how these writers had re-invented themselves in these relationships, thus producing lives that resembled works of art. Some editors thought I would be merely cannibalizing my biographies; others simply thought the material too well worn. They asked, instead, for another biography of a single subject.

Ultimately I decided on what became *The Lives of Norman Mailer: A Biography*. Mailer has adopted many different guises and written about himself in the third person, so he constituted a fitting example of my interest in the ways writers re-create themselves. I had already done work on Mailer's writing, and I felt certain that because two biographies had already been published, he would not try to obstruct my unauthorized effort. The first one, by Hilary Mills, a well-done life, was not a critical biography—that is, other than summarizing reviews, she made no literary assessment of Mailer. The second one, by Peter Manso, was essentially a tape-recorded book, an oral biography skillfully organized. Manso had a falling-out with Mailer—but not before he had interviewed Mailer's mother and most of the key players in his subject's life. Again, however, this book did not deal with the nexus between the work and the life. I proposed a much more interpretative and literary biography, and that is what my publisher, Paragon House, bought.

Mailer had an authorized biographer, Robert Lucid, who is still at work, I believe, on a book that will probably never be published. Lucid once praised a paper I gave on Mailer at a Modern Language Association meeting, and I decided to contact him—hoping that since he held all the cards, he might be generous enough to retrieve a few out of Mailer's vast archive that might be useful for my biography. I presented Lucid with a modest list of requests. He promised to see what he could do, although I never heard from him again. I think he was spying on me and thought I was spying on him, trying to find out how far along he had progressed with his authorized opus. Maybe he thought I had some nerve asking him to act as a reference when I applied for a grant to support the Mailer biography.

Mailer responded courteously to my letters asking for an interview. I was surprised that he did not simply say he had committed himself to Lucid, an old friend, and that therefore he had no time for me. Instead he asked me to send him my Lillian Hellman biography, so that he could assess my writing. Evidently Mailer had forgotten or chose not to acknowledge that he already had one of my books. I had sent him my biography of Marilyn Monroe before it was published, hoping for a blurb from him. His reply noted that he had a pile of books from friends expecting his endorsement and that he could not say he would ever get to mine. He never did—although in 1996 (five years after my Mailer biography appeared) I learned that he knew more about me than he ever disclosed in replies to the letters I sent him in the course of doing his biography. On a visit to the offices *Biography*, which in 1978 had published my article on Mailer's biography, *Marilyn*, Mailer told the journal's editor, George Simson, that my article had been the best discussion of his book that he had ever read.

In 1990, my correspondence with Mailer had to do with the fact that his agent wanted to vet my biography, insisting that if I received permission to quote, such permission would be tantamount to endorsing my biography. I found this position absurd and told Mailer so. He stepped in and not only directed that I be allowed to quote from his work but that I should be charged the lowest possible fee. Perhaps because of his own work as a biographer and authorship of an espionage novel, he took my spying as merely part of the game he himself had been playing for decades.

I wish I could say that episode constituted the happy ending to my work on Mailer. First Peter Manso objected to my editor that I had stolen material from his book. It is true I quoted extensively from Manso's interviews, but they were not his words; he did not own them. He could not claim copyright in these words—as my wife, Lisa Paddock, an attorney, told my editor, who, fortunately, accepted Lisa's argument. Manso made a few more threatening phone calls and then dropped his feeble complaint.

Another controversy ensued when William Styron attempted to recant the testimony he had given for my biography. The contretemps concerned a story Styron told me about an editor (a friend of his and Mailer's) who had stabbed his girlfriend in an incident that occur seven or eight years before Mailer stabbed his second wife, Adele. I tape recorded Styron murmuring how amazed he was to hear Mailer whisper his admiration that the editor had the guts to commit such an act. Mailer and Styron closed ranks, telling the *New York Post* that I had "sensationalized" the story. In fact, I had faithfully reproduced Styron's own wording of the episode and said so to the reporter who duly noted as much in his piece on my biography.

If I seem to digress in this discussion of *The Lives of Norman Mailer*, it is only to emphasize once again the solitude of the unauthorized biographer. Styron had told the story about the stabbing to Hilary Mills. But her version of the story is rather less explicit than mine. Mills was then (and probably still is) a friend of William Styron. He counted on her not to go too far. Why he thought he could count on me, though, is a mystery. A few years earlier I had written him to ask for an interview about Lillian Hellman. He sent a courteous card saying he would like to help but had promised Lillian (practically on her death bed) that he would speak only to her authorized biographer, William Abrahams. Perhaps Styron wanted to be helpful this time, and then had second thoughts, because after our interview he rescinded his offer to grant me access to his archive. Mills, by the way, abandoned a biography of Hellman because she found that even her friends (like Styron) would not consent to interviews about Hellman.

As I was completing my biography of Mailer, I put in a call to Vincent Giroud, curator of Rare Books and Manuscripts at Yale's Beinecke Library. I wanted to see if there had been any changes in the restrictions put on the Rebecca West collection. He informed me that Anthony West had just died. Beginning in the fall of 1991, I started making the trip from New York City to New Haven every Friday to begin the arduous task of reading through an uncatalogued collection of a literary career that spanned over seventy years and a life that lasted to the age of ninety.

I spent nearly a year reading through a good portion of Rebecca's Yale papers, which were a mess. Hundreds of boxes of material had been buried in a Beinecke vault it took a staff member over three hours to locate on my first day trip. Subsequent trips to the Beinecke were almost as frustrating because there was only a rudimentary finding guide to West's papers and only that one staff member seemed to be able to locate items in the order I wanted to follow. But such delays only whetted my curiosity—as did the fact that the guide was not always accurate. I would find the most amazing stuff stuck in those boxes. For example, in the midst of some correspondence from the 1920s, I found a cache of love letters from the 1940s from Francis Biddle (FDR's attorney general and a prosecutor at Nuremberg) to Rebecca.

I thought for sure that anytime that year someone would show up and provide some competition. If anyone had done so, I would have hurried to write my book proposal. In general, I have put together my proposals after about three months of research; in this case, I spent a year researching before submitting a proposal to my agent. The idea of devoting so much time and money on a book that a publisher might not buy and that my agents (in the U.S. and the U.K.) showed no enthusiasm for, struck me as the biggest risk I had ever taken with a book. Much of Rebecca West's work was out of print in the U.S. She had not made it into anthologies taught in college classrooms. Widely read in her own time, she now appeared mainly in the histories and biographies of her period. So why did I persist and take so long in formulating my proposal?

For one thing, my skeptical but tactful agent said that my proposals were so good that she could sell whatever I felt passionately about. And I passionately believed Rebecca West belonged in the canon and that the full story of her life and career had not been told. My Rebecca West proposal would have to be the very best sample of what I could achieve—a pitch not only for my book but also for her. For another, I realized that the Yale collection would provide a significant new cache of material that in itself would be a huge selling point. Finally, I wanted to show just how steeped I was in the archival sources before I began trying to interview people about Rebecca. I had done only American subjects, and I would somehow have to make my way in London literary circles—with some aid, however, from Gellhorn's London friends, who had helped me in spite of her maledictions, and from my London agents. However, I knew no one in Rebecca's family and had no idea how this deeply divided clan (split between those who were related to her son Anthony, whom she had cut out of her will, and her nephew Norman Macleod, who inherited her estate) would react to me.

I had to get the proposal and myself, so to speak, off to a rousing start. I wanted to show, in one paragraph, both the vitality and incredible range of her biography. The first sentence would have to justify my subtitle: A Saga of the Century. Out of Rebecca West I would fashion an emblematic figure:

> The life of Rebecca West (1892-1983) not only spanned a century, it was an invention of a century in the making. In the year before West's birth, George Bernard Shaw published *The Quintessence of Ibsenism*, an argument for a new conception of society and self, socialist in its political orientation, feminist in its demand for equality. Born with the name of Cicily Fairfield (what could sound more Victorian, more like a character satirized by Oscar Wilde?) an eighteen-year-old properly brought up young woman, already steeped in the suffragist struggle, having marched and protested for her rights since she was fourteen and struck in the throat by a policeman during a demonstration, already having failed at a career on the stage, already having died (so to speak) in the throes of adolescent ambition, never minding the pain and ridicule, prepared herself to become a new woman, Rebecca West, Ibsen's defiant heroine, the embodiment of a new age.

I felt I needed to address in a second paragraph the fact that few editors in New York would be familiar with Rebecca's work or have a visual image of her. (Rebecca would more recognizable to London editors but she would not be thought of as bankable, and so I needed a sale in North America first to obtain substantial British backing.) At least Rebecca had appeared in an important film, and her greatest book, *Black Lamb and Grey Falcon*, was still in print, so I tried to anchor a view of her in whatever meager knowledge an editor might already have:

> Rebecca West would be her life long role as a voice of history—as she would come to seem, discoursing on the Russian Revolution in Warren Beatty's film, *Reds*, looking the part she had in fact been awarded in 1959, Dame of the British Empire. This Dame had helped create the era of John Reed and books such as *Ten Days That Shook The World*. In her words, in the chiseled brightness of her sagging but undaunted face, one can trace her passage from Cicily Fairfield, to Rebecca West, to Mrs. Henry Maxwell Andrews to Dame of the British Empire, to the whole woman who was all these things, who plunged into the politics of Central Europe, not at all fazed by the chaos of the Balkans, the upheavals of Yugoslavia that did not merely presage the Second World War, but the world today which is again dividing itself into ethnic enclaves. To remain only a private person, not to engage oneself with world history was, in Rebecca West's view, the equivalent of being an idiot, of not noticing, for example, that the price of peace in the Western world had been bought at the cost of the Eastern Europe's enslavement—first to the Turks and later to the Communists.

Now a third paragraph could work in her agonizing family drama and psychological complexity while emphasizing the Anglo-American trajectory of her career and her cultural and political importance:

> A displaced person herself, part Scotch, part Anglo-Irish, a product of genteel poverty, dark complected and self-conscious about her appearance, West was at home in a world of minorities struggling for self-determination, and an arch opponent of Communism and of every orthodoxy that denied human differences and individual autonomy. She was a marriage of contradictions, a feminist, a mistress, and a dutiful wife, who stood on the margins of society and detected the fault lines running through America and Europe. She partied with Paul Robeson at the Cotton Club in the 1920s and fascinated Huey Long in a famous interview he gave her on the Capital steps in Washington, D.C. She reported on the Nuremberg trials and afterwards set off on the trail of spies and traitors, realizing that betrayal and disloyalty—the things that had split apart her early home life, disrupted her career during her affairs with H. G. Wells and Lord Beaverbrook, and saddened her married years—were the very stuff of history. Not to know about espionage was tantamount to knowing less about one's own life, about the secrets and the lies and duplicities of one's mates and offspring. Her lifelong struggle with her son, Anthony, and her older sister, Lettie, over the meaning of her life, of her relationship with Wells (Anthony's father), was nothing less than an epic engagement over a family's identity, over who Rebecca and Anthony were—not only to each

other but to themselves, to their friends, and to the public which became privy to this familial quarrel, with the roots of it all going right back to Rebecca's ambivalent feelings about her father and mother and to Anthony's sense of illegitimacy.

Rebecca was fascinated with spies and wrote riveting prose about them. She had friends who spied on Anthony, and Anthony had friends who spied on her. I could have made more of that, I see now, re-reading this proposal. A biographer herself, an expert interviewer and confidant with friends in the CIA and the British intelligence services, Rebecca knew the art of deception well and reviewed biographies better than anyone has ever done. But all this I would learn only much later after years of research.

What I did already realize, I'm happy to say, is what a good role-player she was, and how closely her writing and her life coincided. It is as if she gave herself code names and assumed identities:

> In this saga of the century, the political and the personal, the literary and the historical, fuse in the biography of a character named Rebecca West, a character invented once by a playwright and invented again—and again—by the woman herself, who could know herself only by the roles she played, who spent her whole life regretting that she had not stuck to the stage, who wrote a novel, *Sunflower*, casting herself as an actress, who was devastated by her son's novel, *Heritage*, which also cast her in the role of insincere actress, and who finally made it to the screen in *Reds*, speaking not as another's character but as her own, a summation of all the roles and casting calls she had devised for herself.

I doubted that there were many editors who could place Rebecca in literary history and say what her contribution had been. So I supplied a quick overview, being careful to show that she had received critical attention:

> As a novelist, biographer, historian, and critic, who can match West in encompassing so many different forms of expression? As critic Motley F. Deakin remarks, West had an unrivaled command of "libraries of literature"—from the "patristic fathers to the most recent best sellers" and wrote close to a thousand book reviews. Her impact on literary and political journalism was immense, and for a period she divided her time between London and New York, befriending Alexander Woollcott and Harold Ross (she thought of him as a brother) and many *New Yorker* writers, publishing regularly in the *New York Herald Tribune* and *The New Republic* as well as in the most important British newspapers and periodicals. "I doubt whether any such brilliant

reviews were ever seen before; they certainly have not been seen since," wrote Frank Swinnerton in *The Georgian Scene* in an effort to characterize West's influence in the 1920s and 1930s.

But that was a long time ago, and I was keen to build up West not merely as a historical monument but as a timely figure:

> In her biography of St. Augustine she created a figure like herself, deeply self-aware—at the same time extraordinarily self-deluded and capable of creating plots and fictions she was so adept at foiling in others. It is in her autobiographical novels, in the unfinished trilogy that she reveals how her father's abandonment of the family led to a devotion to art which gave back to her a possible world his departure seemed to have denied. In her criticism she spoke of it as the "strange necessity," meaning the peculiar craving for an art that can put a finishing touch to life that life itself lacks. Her accounts of history—particularly of Central Europe—were as necessary as her art. Indeed, she made an art of that history by fusing a displaced peoples' quest for identity with her own, taking her husband along with her as a necessary companion, for he had also had his experience of displacement, having been an Englishman of German heritage interned by Germans in the First World War. "My husband" she is fond of saying in Black Lamb and Grey Falcon as a kind of refrain and backstop to her own perceptions, making out of her marriage a union of disparate ideas. *In The New York Times Book Review* (February 10, 1991), under the front page headline, "Rebecca West: This Time Let's Listen," Larry Wolff shows just how prescient and how relevant West's life and work is for today.

In a last paragraph which concluded the "concept" section of my proposal—a section which is the equivalent of "pitch" screenwriters give when they have an idea for a film—I wanted to convey the idea that justice had not been done to such a profoundly important figure:

> Rebecca West read many languages and wrote in so many different genres that the totality of her achievement has hardly yet been recognized. She turns up as a figure in many books of her period, for she befriended and antagonized and corresponded with the greatest personalities of the twentieth-century: H. G. Wells, Bernard Shaw, Noel Coward, Dorothy Thompson, Diana Trilling, Alexander Woollcott, Paul Robeson, Bernard Berenson, John Gunther, William L. Shirer, Arthur Schlesinger, Jr., Virginia Woolf, Ford Madox Ford, Violet Hunt—the list could go on for pages and pages. And it is in her biography, in the depiction of how Rebecca West became herself, the actress who felt driven to take on so many parts, that the astonishing range of her achievement can be captured. Her career was truly the work of a century.

I then provided an 80-page chapter outline, working in many references to the letters and other documents I had found at Yale and at other archives including the New York Public Library, Boston University, the Library of Congress, the University of Texas and the University of Tulsa. Through Arthur Schlesinger, Rebecca's friend and my colleague at the City University of New York, I had made contact with a few members of her family and could quote them in my proposal. A detailed chronology, an annotated bibliography, an account of published and unpublished biographical resources, and a brief history of how my other biographies had been received rounded out a proposal that ran to 109 pages, about three times as long as my previous ones.

Only a handful of New York trade houses seemed interested in my biography. I did not consider a university press or a smaller publisher because I knew I would never get the kind of advance that would allow me to do the extensive traveling I still needed to do for the book—let alone compensate me for all the expense I had already incurred. Fortunately. Erika Goldman, an editor at Scribner's (a part of the Maxwell empire then and with its apostrophe still intact), bought the book when another eager editor, Don Fehr at Atheneum, could not convince his boss to do so (the boss had edited Victoria Glendinning and could not see the need for another biography). Without Erika, I'm not sure I could have obtained a contract.

My American agent, Elizabeth Frost-Knappman, then showed my proposal to Rivers Scott and Gloria Ferris, Elizabeth's co-agents in London. I had met with them on previous trips to London when they tried to sell my biographies of Gellhorn and Mailer. At one of those meetings sometime in 1988, I had broached the idea of a Rebecca West biography, and Rivers scotched it. He thought it was too soon after Glendinning's book. He mentioned casually that he had known Rebecca, but I did not then inquire further. Now (in early 1992) he told me he had been her editor at the London *Sunday Telegraph*. He also said that Stanley Olson, who had been designated by Rebecca to write an authorized biography much longer than Glendinning's, had died without making any substantial progress on his book. Had I known these facts, I would certainly have put them in my U.S. proposal, since, as I was to learn, Rivers had extraordinary contacts with Rebecca's friends and publishing associates. And as I later discovered from Rebecca's diaries, Rivers had been her favorite editor—more than that, he was a kind of surrogate son. He now helped me tailor my proposal for the British market and won for me a sensational hardback/paperback contract with Hodder & Stoughton, soon to become Hodder Headline. My editor there, the aggressive and brilliant Richard Cohen ran the Cheltenham Literary Festival. But he was promptly fired, and Erika left Scribner's, and my orphaned project passed from one editor to another (seven in all).

However, I felt nothing like an orphan because I had entered a world quite different from those I had ever experienced before as a biographer. I had always been an outsider in every sense of the term. With each biography I had been forced painstakingly to build up a network of contacts, relying chiefly on the way I could put the idea of a book to them and not on whom I knew or who could vouch for me. It was very hard going, and my victories had always seemed miraculous to me. I was astounded, for example, when one day Walter Matthau called me up to talk about Lillian Hellman. I had simply looked up Matthau's professional address in some reference book about actors. As I recall, I had to write to him care of his attorney. I did not expect a reply but felt I had nothing to lose and even suggested to Matthau which days were best to call me! Near the end of our interview, I could not help asking him: "Why did you call me?" "Because," he replied, "you wrote one of the most interesting letters I have read in the last decade." Such responses sustained me, even when I learned Hellman had closed her Texas archive (which had been open for more than 20 years) to all but her authorized biographer, William Abrahams, who had been her editor at Little Brown. Fortunately, a half dozen Ph.D. students had mined that archive before its closure, and I was able to construct much of it from their dissertations. Thus, for me, biography became a primary act of self-assertion, an act of intelligence gathering, and I was determined not to be undone no matter what the obstacle. It was not just a matter of where the sources were; it was always a question of who would be willing to talk to me. If I felt like an outlaw, it was because Martha Gellhorn, for example, had called the Author's Guild in an effort to get them to stop me from writing her biography. Why she thought a writer's organization would be in the business of censoring writers is beyond me, but that tells you something about how odious she assumed I would look to the Guild.

Now, with Rivers's help, I began to feel like an insider. He almost immediately put me in contact with Alan Maclean, who for many years was Rebecca's editor at Macmillan. She liked Maclean and trusted him—a remarkable fact since his brother Donald was part of the famous spy trio that included Guy Burgess and Kim Philby. Alan had nothing to do with spying, but his career had been somewhat blighted by his brother's treason, which had, in part, provoked Rebecca's classic study, *The Meaning of Treason*. She was very keen on the concept of loyalty in both public and private affairs, and she had concluded that Alan deserved her trust. She made him one of her literary executors. I wanted to interview Alan not only about his memories of Rebecca, but also about his contacts in the publishing and literary world that my subject thrived in.

I met Alan not far from my agent's office in a pub on the old Brompton Road in South Kensington. I remember it as a warm enough day for us to sit outside and have a pint. A friendly Alan asked about my previous work. When I mentioned I had published a biography of Lillian Hellman, he ignited. "You know Rebecca and Lillian hated each other," he remarked. He had edited one of Lillian's memoirs but had been careful to steer clear of any conversation about it with Rebecca. This made Alan a kind of double agent, I thought. Perhaps that is why I felt emboldened to raise a subject I probably otherwise would have skirted, especially at this first meeting. "How do you feel about what Rebecca wrote about your brother?" I asked. "Brilliant writing, absolutely brilliant," he replied, "and *wrong*." I did not feel confident enough then to press him on the point. I already knew that Rebecca had keen perceptions and amazing insights, but she could badly misinterpret people she did not like.

Then Alan dropped what felt like a bomb on me. "I'm a good friend of Billy Abrahams, and I promised him I would edit his biography of Lillian when he finishes it." I gulped. I'm surprised I did not choke on my beer. In the preface to my Hellman biography I had mentioned writing to Abrahams asking him to allow me access to Hellman's papers at the University of Texas. Not only did he deny my request, he had gratuitously written that he was the "one and *only* authorized biographer of Lillian Hellman." His response seemed pompous and only made me more truculent and resolute. I had quoted him in the preface and made fun of the idea of a number of biographers who went around claiming to be authorized.[1] Rehearsing this history in my mind I heard Alan say, "Why don't you send me a copy of your Hellman biography? I'd love to read it."

I felt done for. Should I say anything to ameliorate the situation? How would Alan react when he read my outlaw biography? Unauthorized biographies are certainly undertaken in England, but they are deeply discouraged by the literary community and the biographer is often shunned and pilloried in the press—as Stephen Spender's first biographer, Hugh David, had been.[2] To some extent, I

---

1.   Recently I heard Kitty Kelley tell a group of biographers about Frank Sinatra's lawsuit against her. His lawyers claimed to have a tape recording of her saying to an interviewee that she was Sinatra's authorized biographer. When the tape was played for Kelley and her lawyers, it was obvious to her that the voice was not her own. Sinatra's lawyers tried to authenticate the case but obviously could not do so—even after Kelley agreed to allow them to tape record her. Sinatra dropped his suit, but not until his biographer had incurred $100,000 in legal costs.

was, too, when I published a revised biography of Gellhorn in Britain after her death. A dead person cannot sue for libel, and in Britain the onus of proving a book is not libelous is on the author and publisher, whereas in the U.S. the plaintiff has to prove a libel has been committed. Thus far more unauthorized biographies of living figures are squelched in Britain than in the U.S. The stigma of the unauthorized cannot be obliterated—as I found when Michael Foot, who had agreed to my doing a biography of his wife Jill, told me he had received calls from friends doubting the wisdom of allowing me to go ahead. Did not Michael know about my wretched past? Of course he did. He had read and reviewed my biography of Martha Gellhorn, and he and Jill had been very impressed with my biography of Rebecca. But such a reaction in Britain is unusual, and Michael, after all, was a journalist and biographer as well as a politician. He proved to be not quite so open as I supposed when it came to his reaction to my forthcoming biography of Jill—but that is a story to be told another day.

The Guardian launched an attack on my revised biography. I say attack, advisedly, because the reporter included false details—such as that Gellhorn had sued me about the first edition of the biography, and that I had to remove certain objectionable details from the book. The reporter never contacted me—a sure sign that the article was a put-up job. It is true that Gellhorn had a law firm send a threatening letter to my publisher, but there was no lawsuit, and I did not revise any part of the biography because of a court action. *The Guardian* printed my letter of protest, but the damage was done. When my biography was distributed in the U.S., a *Publishers Weekly* reviewer printed the false *Guardian* report in a malicious review—again not bothering to check if I had replied to the British newspaper article. The PW book review editor replied to my email protest, admitting his reviewer had simply repeated the British newspaper report. He published a retraction, but again the damage had been done. Weeks later, at a panel discussion on biography in New York City, an audience member brought up the "fact" that Gellhorn had sued me. Retractions never retract.

"Of course, I'll send you the book," I said to Alan, and said no more. I thought it best for him just to read the biography and let him make up his own mind. I did not want to weight the book with the baggage of explanations. Excerpts from my letters to him during this period explain what happened next:

---

2.   On the subject of authorized and unauthorized biographies, see my *Reading Biography* (New York: iUniverse, 2004 and *A Higher Form of Cannibalism? Adventures in the Art and Politics of Biography* (Chicago: Ivan R. Dee, 2005).

May 14, 1992

Thank you for your letter of May 7. I'm pleased your first impression of my biography is favorable, and I hope it holds up as you read through it…. I do think I would benefit from the designation of "authorised" in that it might, as you say, open a few doors and take care of the permissions problem. Indeed, it would be a great convenience to me now because Tulsa will not photocopy any of West's letters or other unpublished writing without permission from the literary executors.

June 24, 1992

Thank you for your letter of June 17…I'm so pleased you liked the Lillian Hellman biography. Your reaction is what I hoped for, and I'm gratified to say that some of Hellman's friends wrote letters similar to yours.

Whew! Alan never mentioned William Abrahams again. He did, however, express one reservation to Rivers, who relayed it to me. "Do you think," Alan asked Rivers, "an American chap will be able to do right by Rebecca?" Rivers, then in his mid 60s, an affable man and a shrewd negotiator, immediately scoffed at the question. He had read my proposal—better yet, he had massaged it to perfection—and he firmly rejected even the possibility that I might get the story wrong. Agents can do much more than sell a book; the right agent can become a stalwart ally in tight spots.

I don't know, however, if Alan really ever warmed to me. Another American, Stanley Olson, had been designated as Rebecca's biographer of choice. A Midwesterner, Olson had come to London when still a very young man and made himself over into the epitome of an eccentric Englishman. He dazzled the likes of Alan Maclean and the Bloomsbury diarist Frances Partridge. Stanley entertained Rebecca with extraordinary literary gossip he would cull on his rounds in London. A charmer, he must have been a good literary politician, since Frances Partridge and Rebecca did not like each other. Indeed, in the quarrel between Anthony and his mother, Frances took Anthony's side, and Rebecca responded by calling her a "goose down to the last feather."

When I met Alan or Frances or Gwenda David, who worked for Viking in London as a liaison with Viking in New York (Rebecca's American publishers), I sometimes felt their wistfulness. It should be Stanley doing the job, not me. Gwenda, I think, felt his loss most keenly. One day she called up Rivers and complained that I was bothering her. The bother simply had to do with my request for a second interview. Everyone knew I came to get the goods for my biography, and then I would be off. Stanley, on the other hand, had parked himself and would have remained for the long haul. He had planned a ten-year project for a biography of 300,000 words. I was a 150,000 word man and would get the job done in three years at most. Overweight and a gargantuan smoker, Stanley suffered a stroke at 42 (my age when I started my biography of Rebecca) and died a few years later. (I felt I got to know Stanley through his cousin, Phyllis Hatfield, who published a biography of him and with whom I talked frequently, since she, too, had Rebecca stories Stanley had told her.)

Back in the U.S., I still had plenty of work to do at Yale. I had already spent a fortune on photocopying. There was just too much material to take notes on during my one day a week at the Beinecke. I applied for a short-term fellowship that the Beinecke offers to researchers who require an extended period of residence, but I felt I would be successful only if I secured a letter of recommendation from Alan Maclean. He had earlier tried to persuade Yale to open its collection to Victoria Glendinning. Yale refused because of the stipulation that Rebecca had put on the collection regarding her son. That Glendinning was authorized did not change the terms of Rebecca's stipulation. An angry Maclean suspected Yale was upset that Rebecca's substantial collection of literary papers (three times the size of what Yale already had) had been sold to the University of Tulsa rather than given to Yale. At any rate, after first agreeing to write on my behalf, Maclean realized he could not do it. He remained angry about the earlier rebuff. I was left feeling, once again, out in the cold.

I doggedly returned to my one-day-a-week trips to Yale while also fitting in nine research trips to Tulsa, which had a collection three times as large as Yale's. I interviewed Rebecca's friends as well as her son Anthony's family and friends in New York City and in Connecticut. I was able to secure by mail Rebecca's correspondence from various British libraries and archives. But I still had to make nine trips to London and other parts of Britain. One of my best sources, Kitty West, Anthony's first wife, lived a bucolic existence in Dorset. She welcomed my visits and letters and wrote close to two dozen letters filled with her memories of Rebecca and Anthony. Kitty, a remarkable painter and an independent woman, remained in love with Anthony even after he divorced her and remarried. She was on good terms with his second wife, Lily, who could not have been more encouraging to me.

When I first contacted Kitty, however, she said she had received a phone call from someone telling her not to speak with me. The someone was Dachine Rainier, a poet Rebecca had first befriended and then come to regret knowing. Rebecca watched in dread as Dachine proceeded to set herself up as a kind of Rebecca West expert, egging on Viking to do an anthology of Rebecca's work that Dachine would edit and introduce. The publishers did not like Dachine's writing, and Rebecca felt embarrassed by it, but Dachine persisted. Rebecca gradually withdrew from Dachine's company, but her withdrawal did not stop Dachine from publishing reminiscences of Rebecca from time to time. I knew this much from reading Rebecca's correspondence, her diaries, and letters to and from her publishers. I had written to Dachine asking for an interview. She had written me a curt note calling Rebecca a great liar. I, poor chap, would not have a clue as to how to sort out fact from fiction. I drew a line across Dachine's name on my list of people to interview. In retrospect, I can imagine how infuriated she was that an American interloper thought he could just show up and write Rebecca's life.

Of course, I asked Kitty: "What did you say to Dachine?" Kitty replied: "I told her to mind her own business!" Kitty was not in the habit of being instructed as to whom she should see. "Well, that's all right then," I said with a laugh as I fell into a Britishism. Kitty and I liked to stay up late talking about Rebecca and everything else, too. In her very cozy and quiet Dorset cottage I slept the sound repose of the authorized biographer. It was too good to be true. Surely someday I would rue this proximity to my subject, but I never had to. As good as her word, Kitty never asked me to change what I wrote.

After allying myself with Alan Maclean, Kitty, Anthony's family, and then with Alison Macleod—Rebecca's niece who had a treasure trove of family documents and letters—all seemed to be falling in place. Alison had been a Communist and for many years she and Rebecca had fought bitterly. Every time I visited Alison, her husband Jack would remind me, "I used to play chess with Earl Browder [head of the American Communist Party]." Jack was the only one I ever found who called Rebecca Becky, which seemed to amuse her. Alison, was a journalist of considerable accomplishment, who also enjoyed a successful career as an historical novelist. She shares with Rebecca a sarcastic, humorous side that came out when I discussed my research. When I brought up H. G.'s playful letters to Rebecca, whom he called Panther while signing himself Jaguar, Alison commented rather dryly: "They weren't quite human, were they?"

As successful as I had been so far, there was one key witness and center of power, so to speak, that I had to win over: Alison's brother, Norman. I had delayed contacting him because, in a sense, he could make or break my biography. He was Rebecca's heir and chief literary executor. I would need his permission to photocopy the extensive Tulsa files and to quote from Rebecca's writing in my biography. I wanted to quote a good deal because she is such a striking and amusing author.

Norman was also a flashpoint for other members of West's family—especially Kitty, who believed that Anthony had been done out of his inheritance. She found it galling that her two children by Anthony, Edmund and Caroline, received their legacy from Rebecca as administered by Norman. All along, I wondered how I could write a book that would please the Anthony/Macleod sides of the family, especially when what divided them was money!

Norman, is the son of Rebecca's favorite sister, Winifred (Winnie). Norman achieved the higher degrees and settled family life that Anthony (very bad about money) never attempted. Anthony had become a good literary critic and a novelist of indifferent reputation, but he had spoiled his relationship with Rebecca by writing novels and articles about her that made her look like a phony. When Anthony's son Edmund wanted to attend medical school, Rebecca suggested that Anthony contact Norman for advice. It was always Norman! thought a disgusted Anthony. Norman, the paragon of virtue.

So I wondered what Norman was like, this ideal relative who never gave Rebecca trouble. And how would he treat me? I turned to Alan Maclean for help. He wrote to Norman on my behalf, and then Norman invited me to visit him at his cottage in the Lake District. We had a very pleasant visit, and he assured me he liked what I had to say about my approach to Rebecca. There did not seem to be any issue about which he was touchy. He made no stipulations, expressed no demands, and seemed quite content not only to approve my book but also to extend his aid. This he did, for example, by encouraging Anne McBurney, one of Rebecca's secretaries, to speak with me. McBurney had already refused me once.

Even with Norman's encouragement, however, I remained somewhat uneasy. When I asked him about permission to quote from Rebecca's writing, he deferred to Rebecca's agent, Michael Sissons. "So I should apply to Sissons for permission?" I asked Norman. "In the first instance, yes," he said. I remember that phrase distinctly because I did not know what he meant, and rather than pressing him, I decided to see where I stood with Sissons.

I thought he might prove to be another obstacle. I was well along with my book before I met him, and I think he expected writers to apply to him much earlier in the process of their research. In effect, I contacted him with the book half done. I was also wary of him because I knew Rebecca did not like him. She had a decades-long relationship with her agent, A. D. Peters, and Sissons inherited Rebecca when Peters died. It remains unclear to me why Rebecca disliked Sissons (perhaps for no better reason than that he was not Peters), and I did not know if Sissons was aware of her dislike, or whether it mattered to him. I still don't know. There are some questions even I won't ask.

I also worried that Sissons would give me permission but charge a hefty fee for all the quotations I wanted to use. Well, all that worry went for naught, since Sissons turned out to be as obliging as Norman. He simply signed off, so to speak, on my project—although that is only a matter of speaking, since I never obtained, in writing, any sort of permission from Norman Macleod or Michael Sissons. When I completed a presentable draft, I sent it to them and waited to see what they said. I was never charged a thing. Norman pointed out some factual errors and had plenty of comments to make on how Rebecca had chosen to tell her story. Like Dachine, Norman scoffed at some of Rebecca's stories. Rebecca was fond of calling other writers mythomanes, but she did pretty well in that department too. But Norman seemed amused rather than aghast at his aunt's prevarications. And he knew quite well that Rebecca must have been a difficult mother for Anthony. Rebecca was hard on her family and very critical—rarely of Norman, but she certainly had harsh words to say about his wife and other family members. So Anthony's bitterness did not offend Norman, even if Norman did not believe Anthony handled his grievances very well.

On the other side of the water, Anthony's American friends and family felt his anger over his childhood was amply represented in my book. Consequently, I did not suffer from the family conflicts I had anticipated when I first spoke with Kitty. Anthony's son, Edmund, acknowledged his father's paranoid strain, even though Edmund, once Rebecca's favorite, had also experienced her disfavor when he divorced his first wife (a Rebecca favorite) and married his second (a Rebecca bete noir). Everyone in the West family had been insulted by her at some point or felt her sharp tongue had abused a family member.

I found one similarity between Rebecca West and Lillian Hellman. I occasionally contacted people who refused to speak because they felt they could say nothing good about Rebecca or Lillian. In the latter's case, playwright Ruth Goetz refused to be interviewed, but she could not help but whisper fiercely over the phone: "She was a *viper!*" (I have just let out a secret, by the way, because I did not identify Goetz in my biography.) Christina Byam-Shaw, a West relative appalled by Rebecca's treatment of her eldest sister Lettie (or so I heard from other family members) would not meet with me. Here is the approach I took in my third letter to her:

October 8, 1993

Dear Mrs. Byam-Shaw

I feel uncomfortable about not having seen you. I have read various comments about you in Rebecca West's correspondence and in her diaries, and I would like to balance these with an interview with you. I note that Victoria Glendinning thanks you in her acknowledgments, and like Glendinning I will certainly be covering the period during which you knew Rebecca West.

I have conducted more than one hundred interviews with Rebecca West's friends, family, and employees and read more than five thousand of her letters. I am now writing my biography, but I expect to make one more trip to England—probably next autumn when I should have a complete draft but will still be seeing a few people I have missed on previous trips.

Is there any chance we could meet?

I don't believe I got a reply to this third letter. In general, I give up after three tries.

I certainly presented Rebecca's dark side in my biography, but I have never worked on a subject who was more entertaining or who had better friends in spite of her failings. She was generous and amusing and astonishing in her range of interests and in her talents as a writer of journalism, fiction, biography, art criticism, and travel writing.

Did I leave out anything because I was an authorized biographer? Nothing, I do believe, that would have altered my portrayal of Rebecca. Rivers asked me to leave out a bit of Rebecca's diary in which she said she thought of him as a son. He seemed embarrassed by the comment and said his colleagues might make fun of him. To make this confession now reveals the sense in which biography is an intrigue, a keeping and a divulging of secrets.

Above all, Rebecca liked intrigue. I think that is why she found biographies—especially biographies of spies—irresistible. She once criticized contemporary biography as a "blood sport," although she relished the contest between biographer and subject—as her own biographies and reviews of biographies show. Working on her may have increased my own paranoia. My books have always received a high proportion of mixed to negative reviews, with reviewers hostile to my unauthorized approach. Even with my Rebecca West biography, I always thought that in the end I would get the knife, suffer exposure, or be shot attempting to make my escape over the wall every biographer has to climb to get at his subject. In *The Spy Who Came in From the Cold*, Alec Leamas is shot near the Berlin Wall. He could have made it back to the West. But he turned around to try to rescue his companion, a woman he had fallen in love with—although the ruthless Alec would not have used that term. When he looks down from the top of the wall and sees his love has been shot, he descends and gets hit.

Like Alec Leamas, I have been a loner. So it came as a delightful surprise when reviewers almost uniformly approved of my biography—including Victoria Glendinning, who might have seen me as a sort of rival. I have made relatively few friends out of the contacts I have made when researching my subjects. Rebecca West, however, has been an exception. She brought me friends like Michael Foot, Jill Craigie, Kit Wright (she hosted Rebecca during her stays in Mexico), and many others, including virtually all of Rebecca's family (who I continue to see and who visit me). They provide a degree of warmth I have not otherwise experienced as a biographer. For better or worse, I've always been one of those biographer/spies who does not look back.

REBECCA WEST'S POLITICS: A BIOGRAPHER'S PERSPECTIVE

This essay is an outgrowth of a talk that I gave at the first annual Rebecca West Conference, held in New York City at the Mercantile Library in the fall of 2003. It will appear, as well, in different from as a preface to a new collection of essays about West to be published by the University of Delaware Press.

This essay is as much about biography as it is about Rebecca West's politics. A biographer herself, West would have approved of my approach, if not necessarily of my conclusions. She saw biography as a primary source of knowledge. She objected strenuously to T. S. Eliot's attempt to expunge the writer's personality from his work.[1] At heart, she was a Romantic, projecting her own personality into history. This is evident in her masterpieces, *Black Lamb and Grey Falcon* and *Survivors in Mexico*. But it is true also of *The Meaning of Treason*, *A Train of Powder*, and her other nonfiction and fiction.

Writing from a biographer's perspective means drawing upon dozens of interviews with West's family, friends, enemies, and casual acquaintances. Of course, I am also relying on her letters and manuscripts, many of which are autobiographical. In the end, however, I am writing as my own authority—the kind of authority R. G. Collingwood had in mind when he rejected the idea that history was a compilation, a matter of scissors-and-paste, a collage of materials gathered from disparate sources. The complete historian, according to *The Idea of History*, absorbs his sources and transcends them.

Academics often assemble their writing as scissors-and-paste history by presenting a formidable array of footnotes—as if what they write is settled by cita-

---

1. See Rebecca West, "Tradition in Criticism." *Tradition and Experiment in Present-Day Literature* (1929): 179-97. Reprinted in the forthcoming iUniverse collection, *Woman as Artist and Thinker*.

tion. If that were so, academic disputes would be at an end. After all, just look at the documentation. In fact, the most important part of any argument cannot be footnoted.

Rebecca West rarely footnoted. Her voice constituted her authority. When she described William Joyce's jaunty walk in *The Meaning of Treason*, she wrote a scene based on what his family and friends had told her, but every sentence about Joyce derived from her experience as biographer, which could not be reduced to a source note.

Much the same can be said about West's politics. As a political person she is more than the sum of her writings or of what people said about her, and more than what is in her letters and manuscripts. When I write about West's politics, I have in mind the whole person as I have come to imagine her over the past fifteen years. There is no way to bring her politics alive without doing something like what a novelist does: conceive of a character. Undoubtedly, what I conceive—no matter how much it is based on documentation—is a construct, one that no one could duplicate without having gone through the biographer's experience. Otherwise, why read biography at all? The biographer, shorn of his symbiotic relationship with his subject, is just become another critic. That would make T. S. Eliot happy, but not Rebecca West, who wanted to know not only what William Joyce thought, but how he *moved* and about the world he moved in, and then project all of that through the screen of her own sensibility.

West provided the key to understanding her politics when she wrote that by the age of five she understood the meaning of political terms such socialism and anarchism. In her household, politics was served up as regularly as the meals; it took the form of daily debate.[2] She had a journalist father who brought home Russian revolutionaries. There was a lot of crazy talk, and there is no question that Rebecca thought it demented. Perhaps any five-year-old would. But not every five-year-old grows up to be Rebecca West and writes *The Birds Fall Down*, which is in part her memory of those wacky radicals she watched argue with her reactionary father. How could anyone suppose such goofs would come to rule the world? Any perceptive child knew better—or perhaps it took a child—not yet corrupted by cant—to see the truth.

The child's eye view, so important to classics like *Great Expectations* and *Huckleberry Finn*, is what motivates *The Fountain Overflows*. In this supreme work of fiction, West wanted to show how her narrator, a child-woman, comprehends, at

---

2.   See Carl Rollyson, *Rebecca West: A Saga of the Century* (1996): 23-25 and *The Literary Legacy of Rebecca West* (1998): 2-3, 7-8.

a very early age, the nature of the world—even before she can articulate it. Although she adores her father, she also sees in him a malign spirit attracted to the corrupt world outside the home. He is a gambler who destroys his aesthetic sensibility as well as his commitment to his family, which has been his anchor, but which he abandons to his doom.

In her family memoirs, Rebecca West was never able to get much beyond her own eighth year when her father deserted the family. And it is hard for me to get beyond thinking about how her sense of politics intensified in the crucible of her father's flight from home. Her political precocity demands the biographer's attention. How many others in this world can attach such an early date to the dawning of their political consciousness? And what happens to you when you are exposed so early to political discussion and find you have no trouble understanding it?

I can date my own political awakening to 1960, when I was 12 and John Kennedy ran for president. In junior high school a demanding teacher was shocked that no one in class could recall the Suez crisis of 1956. I was then eight and do not remember it at all. But think of a Rebecca West who could vividly recall Queen Victoria's jubilee and the Boer War—events that occurred before her eighth year. It is no accident that her last completed book should be titled *1900*, for that year was the *sine qua non* of her family and political life, when her domineering father abdicated his role. That betrayal would fuel her lifelong obsession with families and political movements infected with treachery.

It is not an exaggeration to say that by the age of eight Rebecca West already understood that an event like the Russian Revolution would be doomed—a revolution that would not occur for another sixteen years. Although she went to Fabian summer school and shared the socialist vision of a new society, she never exhibited the slightest enthusiasm for the Bolshevik ascent to power. Indeed, her writing during 1917-1918 shows that she did not believe the Revolution would respect human rights or, in the long run, survive except as corrupt, duplicitous regime.[3] That she embraced Emma Goldman in the early 1920s, seconding that revolutionary's attack on Soviet tyranny, seemed premature to H. G. Wells, George Bernard Shaw, and even to Conservatives like Lord Beaverbrook who accepted the Soviet Union as a disagreeable reality.[4] George Orwell has often been lauded for his prescience about totalitarianism. But Rebecca West was decades ahead of him and virtually everyone else on the left.

---

3. *Rebecca West: A Saga of the Century*: 63; *The Literary Legacy of Rebecca West*: 29.
4. *Rebecca West: A Saga of the Century*: 105-08.

West responded not merely to the ideas of revolutionaries but to their affect. She understood their psychology. They lived in a hermetic, paranoid world. The only novelists in the Anglo American world who preceded West in their awareness that these revolutionaries would wreck the world because of their insularity and unstable natures were Henry James and Joseph Conrad—two early influences on West. *The Princess Cassimassima* and *The Secret Agent* should have been beacons to modern writers involving themselves in radical politics. When West wrote a series of pieces about Stalin for the *Evening Standard* January 28-February 1, 1952), she emphasized his seminary background and the spying and conspiratorial behavior he absorbed in such an institution. He learned, in other words, to be a great criminal.[5]

When as a young woman West rejected her father's reactionary politics and became a radical feminist and socialist, she envisioned a world in which women would claim their equal right to shape political institutions and force men to share power. The only effective way to change the world was through democratic reforms. Protests—even violent protests—she could support. But the idea of overthrowing governments appalled her—although she had to admit that without the example of the French Revolution to inspire her, Emmeline Pankhurst might well not have conceived of the drive for women's liberation which centered on securing votes for women, which in turn would lead to a transformation of a legal code that disadvantaged women as wives and workers.[6]

But early on West also realized that socialist politics were not, in practice, democratic at all. The male dominated unions did not share power with women, so how could they ever be trusted to create a society in which women had their equal role to play? Even worse, England's homegrown socialism failed to evolve—in part because of the leftist fascination with Red Russia.[7] The Soviet model was irrelevant, if not pernicious, West told her leftist friends. But few listened, since to act upon West's advice would mean ostracism—a marginalization that West herself felt keenly and which did untold damage to her literary reputation—as I have shown in "Rebecca West and the God That Failed."

---

5.   For more commentary on West's overlooked incisive biography of Stalin, see *Rebecca West: A Saga of the Century*: 285.

6.   For the parallels between Emmeline Pankhurst and Rebecca West, see Carl Rollyson, "A Conservative Revolutionary: Emmeline Pankhurst (1857-1928)" (2003): 325-34.

7.   See Rebecca West's introduction to Emma Goldman, *My Disillusionment with Russia* (1924).

When Sylvia Pankhurst and other socialists and union members refused to support World War I, West deplored their actions as self-destructive. She applauded Emmeline Pankhurst's pro-war stance. Did leftists think the Germans, if they won the war, would liberate women and create a socialist society? Of course, Britain had to be defended. Emmeline Pankhurst's fate after World War I is instructive for a student of West. Mrs. Pankhurst watched her own daughter Sylvia flirt with Leninism, thus weakening the drive for reform in Britain. Mrs. Pankhurst also recalled that most Labor Party members—the great Keir Hardie excepted—had done little to advance the woman's cause. And the unions were just as obstructive. Unlike West, though, she actually moved toward the Conservative Party. West, on the other hand, did not mind entertaining Conservatives in her own home—or going to bed with them as in the case of Lord Beaverbrook—but as *Black Lamb and Grey Falcon*'s epilogue shows, she always thought of herself as the conscience of the left—although she never herself used such self-important language to describe herself.

To West, the 1920s and 1930s revealed that the left had a death wish. Whatever failings the Conservatives had, at least they wanted to rule and to exercise power. The left, on the other hand, would rather be right, and would rather preserve its ideological purity, than expose itself to the complications and contradictions of political office. The short-lived Labor governments of this era seemed paralyzed, afraid to make any move that would cause controversy and seemed to be relieved when they were voted out of office.

West supported the left's efforts to save the Spanish Republic during the Spanish Civil War, even though she realized that Stalin's agents had co-opted the Republican cause. She even funded a radical like Ralph Bates to tour the U.S. and drum up support for the anti-fascist fighters in Spain. Bates was grateful, but when I interviewed him in the 1990s near the end of his life, he was reluctant to make his involvement with her part of the record and, indeed, asked me to take his account out of my biography. He never said why, but as Doris Lessing told me, West's fierce criticisms of the left, her marriage to what people supposed was a Conservative banker, had made her a pariah in progressive circles.

But West's husband, Henry Andrews, was hardly the typical English gentleman. In fact, he was hardly English at all. She made a point of his unEnglishness in her unfinished memoirs—at one point even wanting to put the story of his family first—the idea being that like her he was a displaced person and for all his banking background and tweed suits and Rolls Royce, he only played at being a country squire. In fact, he was no good at it. West emphasized his scholarly mind, not his business acumen (of which she felt he actually had less of than her).

When West married Andrews in 1930, Virginia Woolf and the Bloomsbury set thought Henry a bore, simply a trophy husband for a woman in her late 30s who was tired of consorting with the younger set and wanted a man to take care of her. There is some truth in that distorted picture, but not very much. Henry was at the forefront of anti-fascism. He had seen Nazi brutality firsthand as an employee of a German bank. He spirited many Jews out of Germany at considerable risk to his own life.

To me the most telling story about Henry came from his farm manager, Harold Tomlinson, who remembered the great Labor landslide of 1945. West wrote two articles for *Harper's* (September and November, 1945) lauding Churchill as a great war leader but stipulating that he would not do for peacetime. The people were restless and ready for fundamental changes in the structure of society. Churchill, still glorying in the Empire and trying to hold on to India, was not likely to deliver this new world—what came to be known as the welfare state. Henry went round to the staff of Ibstone, the country home he and Rebecca had bought before the war, to encourage them to vote Labor. Henry may have enjoyed this sort of Lord of the Manor role, but his farm manager did not resent it or even think it out of character for Henry to advocate a Labor vote. Tomlinson saw Rebecca as much more businesslike than Henry, who seemed to have trouble telling time and keeping appointments. It was easy to make fun of Henry and to suggest he was out of it and a rather precious imbecile to boot. West's niece, Alison Macleod, told me of an incident in which Henry expressed surprise that her daughter had taken a bus to some event. "Oh," Henry said in his perfectly modulated argot, "I did not know one could arrive by public conveyance." Alison's brother, Norman, scoffs at such stories. This is not the shrewd Henry he knew.

Just as her father brought home his political opponents and would defend the political rights of Catholics even though he disliked Catholics, West sought out people from every level of society—which made interviewing a fascinating journey from her hairdresser to William F. Buckley, Jr. What other modern writer had friendships that ranged from Emma Goldman and Paul Robeson to Francis Biddle, FDR's attorney general and a Nuremberg judge and Allen Dulles, director of the CIA?

There is no doubt that as West grew older she found more of a welcome among Conservatives than Liberals, although plenty of the latter like Arthur Schlesinger remained fond of her in spite of disagreements about McCarthyism and anti-Communism. In fact, it is West's stance as a virulent anti-Communist that ruined her reputation among the left. Even those who had admired her journalism—like Martha Gellhorn—turned against West in the 1950s and stopped reading her.[8]

The trouble began with a series of articles about McCarthyism published in *U.S. News and World Report*, then considered to be a conservative organ. West pointed out that the articles had been bought from a British paper, and that she had no control over their publication in America. More importantly, however, was her refusal to rebuke Senator McCarthy. While not giving him a ringing endorsement, her failure to condemn him infuriated liberals and led to an argumentative exchange with Arthur Schlesinger and other liberals—a brouhaha I detail in my biography (pp. 284-94).

During this controversial period, West received many letters from intimate friends like the writer Emanie Arling, who attempted to explain the kind of havoc McCarthy had caused. Writers lost jobs because they were suspect Communists or fellow travelers. In short, it was the era of the blacklist. West was not impressed, and that is a puzzle.

After all, West had championed Emma Goldman not only because she had the courage to denounce the Soviet regime but also because Goldman had been unjustly deported from the United States. West deplored the infamous Palmer Raids, the rounding up of radicals in America instigated by attorney general Palmer. Lives were ruined and careers damaged because people were labeled Reds. It is curious, by the way, that while West appeared in Warren Beatty's film *Reds*, she said nothing about this aspect of the period the director dramatized. Or was that aspect of West's commentary cut from the film? Although I tried to get Warren Beatty to answer that question, my attempts to contact him proved futile.

Why did West not see a parallel between the Palmer Raids and McCarthyism? I have no definitive answer, but my surmise is that history had made a difference. By the 1950s, West had witnessed more than two decades of Communist apologetics—a generation of intellectuals eager to condone any Communist atrocity such as the Moscow trials of old Bolsheviks and the Hitler-Stalin pact. And West herself had become a target for Communists and fellow travelers who labeled her a reactionary because of her virulent anti-Communism. Liberals like Isaiah Berlin and Noel Annan—influential opinion makers in Britain and America—shied away from West and suggested she was just too extreme.[9] It was all well and good

---

8.　The trajectory of Martha Gellhorn's response to West is a good barometer of liberal opinion. See my biography, *Beautiful Exile: The Life of Martha Gellhorn* (2003): 244-47.

9.　See *The Literary Legacy of Rebecca West*: 189-91.

to be anti-Communist, they said, but West and her American ally, Diana Trilling, had become monomaniacs on the subject. In other words, West felt not merely isolated but positively blackballed herself—not that she could not publish but that what she published was immediately dismissed and often not read by the left.

Thus it is not so surprising that West thought the reaction to McCarthy was overwrought and out of proportion to the crimes Communists had committed abroad and the subversive activities they practiced at home. She had no doubt that Alger Hiss, the Rosenbergs, and Elizabeth Bentley, for example, were spies and disloyal citizens. But she could not reveal that she was receiving files from the House Committee on UnAmerican Activities (HUAC) that confirmed her suspicions.

HUAC has often been dismissed as a grandstanding politically conservative body bent on destroying the legacy of the New Deal and hence of liberalism per se. HUAC's harping on the Communist Conspiracy was merely a weapon against the Democratic Party. In retrospect, it is clear that while HUAC was often venal, it did produce valuable research that as deep background found its way into many of West's newspaper articles. The charge that HUAC was a fraud because its investigations did not lead to convictions is not as devastating as its opponents would like to think. As a recent biography of the "Red Spy Queen," Elizabeth Bentley, shows, the Soviet Union was rolling up its spy networks by the time HUAC got started, and many of the spy rings, which Bentley exposed, had destroyed a good deal of evidence that could have been used to convict them. And then, of course, there was the fact—as in the Rosenberg case—that the government had difficulty securing convictions because it did not want to divulge its sources and compromise its own security investigations.[10]

West knew this intricate structure of national security better than any other writer in the Western world.[11] Her husband had been a close friend of Allen Dulles since the 1930s. West had close contacts with British security agencies. At one time the Director of Public Prosecutions, Theobald Mathew, was her personal attorney. Even more importantly, West understood how bureaucracy worked. It could be inefficient and unjust, but no government could function without internal security institutions. This insight makes her reading of Kafka in *The Court and Castle* one of the most original and well-informed interpretations

---

10. See Lauren Kessler, *Clever Girl: The Spy Who Ushered in the McCarthy Era* (2003). I reviewed this book in *The New York Sun*, August 27, 2003, p. 15.
11. See "Rebecca West and the FBI," included in this volume.

of that great writer. She pointed out that he had worked for government, and that his view of bureaucracy was much more nuanced and paradoxical than liberals and radicals understood. Kafka had not written just to condemn modern government. Far from it. He wrote as a deeply engaged participant in the making of the modern political world. This is not to deny, however, that in the end Kafka becomes a good deal like West in his political orientation. Like all great Romantics, West half perceived and half created the world she wrote about.

Government was not the main enemy, in West's view. By focusing so much attention on McCarthy, liberals lost sight of what their government had to contend with: a determined group of men and women who hid behind the fifth amendment and lied about their Communist affiliations. HUAC was often criticized for humiliating witnesses and for making them "name names" when HUAC already had the names. But as West knew, HUAC was attempting to build a case that would not have to rely on government security reports. To a great extent, the Communist effort to stonewall HUAC was successful, and then that success was used against HUAC to proclaim that it could not prove its charges.

That West stood her ground and refused to make McCarthy the main issue is one of the great moments of her career, although, in a sense, it cost her her career. It disabled her as an influential voice among the left. So injured did she feel that even in old age, when she was writing her Sunday book reviews for the *Telegraph*, she begged off reviewing a book that would have revived the painful period when she lost a good deal of her influence in America and Great Britain.

Rather than continuing to make her point in nonfiction, West dealt with the Communist menace in *The Birds Fall Down*, a best seller in 1966. To me this is a prophetic novel because it shows why the Russian Revolution was doomed from the start. West wisely set her book more than a decade before 1917 so that she could deal with the roots of the Revolution without having to battle critics who would undoubtedly accuse her of a conservative attack on the revolution itself. As in *The Fountain Overflows*, the center of consciousness is a young woman. Indeed, *The Birds Fall Down* is the political complement to *The Fountain Overflows*. Together these two novels represent West's fusion of art and politics, her concerns with social justice, the role of the artist, and of the politically conscious individual. Her two female heroines become the focal point of her feminism, and these two novels recapitulate and ramify a sensibility that nearly 70 years earlier was in embryo as a young girl who watched her father bring the world home to her.

REBECCA WEST AND THE
GOD THAT FAILED

*This article was first published in the Wilson Quarterly. I expected to receive some
hostile responses taking issue with West's anti-Communism. But the journal's editor
assured me that the response was virtually unanimously positive. How history changes.*

In 1950, Arthur Koestler and five other writers published *The God That Failed*,
six accounts explaining how they came to join or to fall within the orbit of the
Communist Party. They had in common a sense of outrage at injustice and a
rebellious need to identify with a cause and an ideology that represented, they
thought, the wave of the future, a God to whom they could tender their absolute
devotion. At this late date—after many memoirs like *The God That Failed*—there
is little need to rehearse why it is that these writers became disillusioned with
Communism. We have a literature of debates about Dos Passos's shift from left
to right, the testimony of those who recanted their Communism before HUAC,
and more recently, Susan Sontag's apostasy in 1982, accompanied by her coinage
of Communism as Fascism with a human face.[1] If Francis Fukayama's phrase
about the end of history means anything, it is that the God not only failed, it is
dead. The future that Communism supposedly foreshadowed, and Communism
as an interpretation of history, have perished.

In memoirs such as *The God That Failed* we have been schooled to believe in a
paradigm—let us call it the Arthur Koestler intellectual, a true believer in the
Communist utopia whose disenchantment leads him to an apocalyptic vision of
darkness at noon. The trouble with the paradigm is that it concedes that at some
point, however briefly, Communism was a seductive ideal. We expect the twentieth-century intellectual, except for the staunchly conservative thinker, to be
enticed—even corrupted—before he or she recovers and bears witness in the

---

1.   Not quite as good as Rebecca West's quip that Communism was Fascism with a
     "geographical and glandular difference."

manner of Whittaker Chambers, the controversial ex-Communist agent who exposed the espionage of Alger Hiss, a former State Department official..

But what of Rebecca West? She occupies a position that is highly unusual, if not unique. She had the honor, and also the misfortune, to declare Communism a dud as early as 1918—even before Lenin had consolidated his power. She was only twenty-five-years old, the author of *The Return of the Soldier* (1918), a classic of World War I fiction, and of *Henry James* (1916), an incisive and witty study that helped to place that author in the canon. George Bernard Shaw observed that his British colleague handled a "pen as brilliantly as ever I could and much more savagely." As early as 1912, she had been taken under the wing of H. G. Wells, Ford Madox Ford, and the Fabian Socialists. As a militant feminist, she had rocked the Edwardian world with her savage and witty essays in *The Free-woman,* a radical weekly.[2] Indeed, her pseudonym, taken from the radical heroine in Ibsen's play, *Rosmersholm,* embodied the cause of political protest and seemed a desirable alternative to Cicily Fairfield, her impossibly genteel family name.

If West displayed a prescient independence of mind, it was largely because the world of ideas was a part of her life from her earliest years. She was born in London but educated at George Watson's School in Edinburgh. At sixteen a bout of tuberculosis ended her schooling, yet she never really regretted her lack of a university degree, saying she could not remember a time when she did not have a "rough idea of what is meant by capitalism, socialism, individualism, anarchism, liberalism, and conservatism." Her Scottish mother, Isabella, an accomplished pianist with an acerbic wit, often took her to public lectures, and both of her two older sisters became involved in the Fabian movement. She learned very early how to take the measure of people and their ideas. Her conservative father, an Anglo-Irish journalist named Charles Fairfield, brought home intellectuals, artists, and politicians, including several Russians. She saw then, as she said later, that Marxism was just another "rainbow. *Das Kapital* is a dreary book, except for that chapter of wild praise for the achievements of the bourgeoisie." Her father had been tutored by the Reclus brothers, anarchists thrown out of France. Her family were friends with many Russian refugees and revolutionaries who came to argue with Charles Fairfield and to be shrewdly observed by his precocious daughter. She knew at eight what socialists like the Webbs never figured out: that it would not do to patronize the Bolsheviks. She knew they were much more cul-

---

2.   As H.G. Wells quipped, the journal "existed it seemed chiefly to mention everything a young lady should never dream of mentioning."

tivated and more on the spot and more dangerous and more sophisticated than the Webbs. That realization "rather cut me off from the left-wing movement of my time," West drily remarked.

But West's views did not turn her into a young fogy of the right. She flayed the conservative opposition throughout the teens and twenties, irreverently suggesting, for example, that Prime Minister Asquith would make an excellent butler. Her first article trumpeted her defiance of the status quo in blunt language rarely employed by male writers—let alone by a woman not quite nineteen years of age: "There are two kinds of imperialists—imperialists and bloody imperialists."

Yet never for a moment did West consider the 1917 revolution the harbinger of hope. To this day, significant elements of the Left have never forgiven her for being correct. Her position cost her friends and earned her enmity. It was damned indecent of her not to have had at least some initial enthusiasm for the great experiment.

But this is to get ahead of her story, one that is not widely known or understood. The common impression of her is that after starting out well as a flaming feminist and socialist, and in 1914 bearing a son, Anthony West, out of wedlock with H.G. Wells, West let her side down: she turned conservative, married a rich man in 1930, retired to a country estate, and in her last years supported Margaret Thatcher. In other words, West is consigned to the left-to-right slot.

In fact, Rebecca West never deserted the Left; it was the Left that repudiated her. In late 1917, as reports filtered into England about the Bolshevik seizure of power, West wrote disdainfully of the revolutionary movement's "orgiastic loquacity."[3] A year earlier, she had denounced the trade unions for seeing things only in terms of the class struggle and ignoring the German invasion of Belgium and the threat to England. She believed in national purposes and traditions—not in supranational ideologies that led, as she later argued in *The Meaning of Treason* (1948), to the betrayal of rational, democratic values.

Yet West never willingly parted company with socialists, arguing in 1918 for the election of the Labor Party, although she worried that it was most interested in purity of principle that is easier to maintain as a political minority than as the

---

3.   Nearly fifty years later in her novel *The Birds Fall Down* (1966), she would make this loquacity a symbol of the revolutionary's revocation of a sense of reality by finding refuge in solipsistic speechifying. V.S. Pritchett teased West about her voluble characters, saying they "majored in being Russian." But that was her point: the revolution was no real revolution, it was merely Russian.

governing majority. She refused to hew to a party line, and she would not countenance any winking at tyranny in the Soviet Union. One of her finest moments of intellectual integrity came in 1924 when anarchist Emma Goldman visited England. West admired Goldman's campaigns in the United States for freedom of speech, and now Goldman sought to awaken the British Left to Soviet atrocities. West lined up speaking engagements for her, made sure that she met Bertrand Russell, H. G. Wells, and many prominent socialists. The Left at first feted Goldman but then quarantined her when she made it clear that the Soviet system could not be ameliorated. It was not just a matter of protesting this or that failing of Communism, it was time to junk it, Goldman argued. But this is what the Conservative Party recommended! gasped the Left. West responded with a preface to Goldman's *My Disillusionment with Russia* (1923), observing that to "reject a conclusion simply because it is held by the Conservative party is to be snobbish as the suburban mistress who gives up wearing a hat or dress because her servant has one like it." To pretend that the Soviet Union was a "conscientious experiment in Communism" was sentimental rubbish, West declared, and socialists who shut their eyes to its evils degraded the socialist movement, which would rot from within, she predicted, if it did not oppose a government that deprived its citizens of the "elementary rights of free speech and assembly." Neither Goldman nor West advocated intervention in Soviet affairs: "We must let each people seek God in its own way," West proposed. Her concern was that in propping up the Soviet Union as a positive model, socialists would lose their credibility, their ability to reckon with "real facts," and become "tedious liars about life."

Isn't this precisely what happened? Didn't the Left discredit itself by wilfully ignoring, or rationalizing, or denying Soviet oppression? It angered West that the British, who had developed their own tradition of socialism, should enslave themselves to apologetics for the Soviet model. The Left was behaving as provincially as the suburban housewife when it had a body of thought of its own to mine and refine. West *wanted* to believe in a socialist future—but not at the price of sacrificing a sense of reality. She was once invited to dinner at the home of Sidney and Beatrice Webb, the Fabians' patron saints, but she was never asked back because of her critical tongue. Later, she had only scorn for the Webbs' paeans to the Soviet Union.

West's early and persistent criticism of Communism cost her dearly. Doris Lessing wrote to me that West was consistently and bravely critical of communism, at a time when this meant she was subject to the usual denigration and slanders. I remember it all too well. It wasn't just a question of "the comrades" but a climate of opinion which extended far beyond the extreme left. Orwell was a target and so was Rebecca W. It must have been hard to stand up to it, particularly as she was sensitive and hated being considered negligible, yet she did, standing by her guns. And of course she was right, and her critics so very wrong.

How should you know all that? It must seem a long time ago to you, and I do know that the hardest thing in the world is to understand a "climate of opinion" when it has gone and even seems faintly ridiculous. Well, that climate was poisonous.

That climate has not entirely gone, I might add. When I began work on my biography of West in 1990, I was puzzled at the paucity of good work on her. Other than Victoria Glendinning's excellent short biography,[4] there are reviews, a few introductory studies, a handful of perceptive articles, but no in depth study of this major twentieth-century writer. There are many reasons for this neglect, and one of them surely is her politics.

In academic circles, it has been quite all right to approve West's early socialist articles under the title *The Young Rebecca*, but her mature work, has been ignored. This imbalance has contributed to the myth of West's left-to-right trajectory. Neither her writing nor her biography supports the myth, and a close examination of both bursts the sentimental version of "The God That Failed" story, of the intellectuals who just had to identify with Communism and then recant. This story is simply not true—not for West, and not for her great contemporary in France, Raymond Aron, the closest parallel I can find to West's truly independent and intellectual stance.

West was never comfortable in any camp. Although she wanted a home on the Left, she was never willing to play by the house rules. She thought Stalinism a greater threat than McCarthyism, and when she said so in 1953, her series of articles in *U.S. News and World Report* was subjected to a firestorm of criticism from liberals. If West did not fiercely attack McCarthy, she was regarded as pro-McCarthy and conservative. But to the hysterical claims about the danger of McCarthyism (she conceded McCarthy did abuse the system), she replied that

---

4.   Glendinning's *Rebecca West: A Life*, published in 1987 by Knopf, was supposed to be followed by a fuller biography, to be written (at West's request) by Stanley Olson. But Olson died before he had done much research or writing, and I decided to write the second biography after West's Yale archive was opened in 1989.

focusing on him merely diverted attention from the menace of the Communist conspiracy. He was not murdering anti-Communists—the Communists were.[5] And in Europe the myth of McCarthyism was used as an anti-American weapon to suggest that America now had a dictator, the puffed-up senator from Wisconsin.

West wrote an admiring review of Whittaker Chambers's *Witness* (1952), but unlike him she could not embrace the conservative cause.[6] She shied away from William F. Buckley Jr.'s invitations to write for *The National Review*, although she was his guest and often his sympathetic reader. Early on, she was one of Winston Churchill's fiercest opponents, finding him to be a politician without principle, saying that his career proved that there were some souls for whom the devil did not care to pay a price. Yet she gloried in his prosecution of the war, saying he had brought back the age of the Elizabethans. Like the majority of British voters at the end of the war, she voted him out of office, believing he had served his usefulness. Yet even as she voted in a Labor government, she was highly critical of it in her private letters and conversations, just as she criticized big government corruption in the New Deal while at the same time praising the Roosevelts' efforts to lead the nation.

What appealed to West was patriotism—not mindless loyalty, but a critical devotion to the national ideal. She once wrote that every nation should be chauvinistic in the sense that it should believe it has something unique to contribute to the world—but, she added, thank God the whole world was not England or, perish the thought, the Soviet Union! Not enough readers have been exposed to the biting humor and the wisdom of such remarks—too many of which are still buried in periodicals, having never appeared between hard covers.[7]

---

5.   West's main criticism of McCarthy was ignored. She did not worry that he was giving anti-Communism a bad name. She thought reports of liberals losing their jobs and becoming blacklisted exaggerated. The real danger in McCarthy's tactics, she argued, was that he was recklessly attacking the federal bureaucracy and weakening a faith in government. She did not see how modern life could be governed without bureaucracies, and while she supported their reform, she distrusted politicians who seemed to run against the government itself.

6.   Chambers wrote most of the 1947 *Time* cover story on West and is the author of the most trenchant observation about her temperament: "Rebecca West is a Socialist by habit of mind, and a conservative by cell structure."

7.   The International Rebecca West Society plans to begin republishing West's important periodical work, beginning with a collection of articles, entitled *"Woman as Artist and Thinker."*

Rebecca West lacked the tactical and temperamental sense to acquire acolytes or to attach herself to movements like Bloomsbury. She despised Communists for their log rolling and cronyism and applauded efforts to root them out of the Washington bureaucracy. She felt the same way about Communist writers and fellow travelers who created the climate of opinion Doris Lessing deplores. She turned her corrosive and uncompromising wit on friends as well as on enemies. At *Time and Tide*, a British weekly West published in for more than three decades, a colleague observed (anonymously): "It is probable that if there is ever an English Revolution there will come a point when the Reds and Whites will sink their differences for ten minutes while they guillotine Miss West for making remarks that both sides have found intolerably unhelpful." Her editor at the *Evening Standard* remarked that people saw her as a "caustic, bitter, twisted woman with a tongue like broken glass, fierce, mocking, inhuman." When she was covering the Fascist riots in post World War II London, there came a moment when she was booed by both Communists and Fascists, a moment she relished.

West's hostile readers might want to dismiss her as a career anti-Communist who at best has served her purpose and is only of historical interest. But in addition to her considerable legacy as a novelist, literary critic, and biographer, there is a political body of thought that deserves book-length treatment. Her masterwork, *Black Lamb and Grey Falcon* (1941), is a monumental study of Yugoslavia, but it is also her definitive pronouncement on feminism, marriage, the history of Europe, and of Western Civilization. The breakup of Yugoslavia, for example, would not have surprised her, for she realized that although Tito had suppressed national and ethnic rivalries, he did not eradicate them. Indeed, Communism, with its bogus internationalism, attempted to deny people their heritage—not just the national political rights of Serbs, Croats, and Muslims, but of Macedonians, Albanians, Hungarians, Italians, and Slovenes.

For Rebecca West, history could not be understood in terms of ideology, of ideas that could be superimposed on tradition. Instead, she allied herself with writers such as Burke and De Toqueville, precisely those thinkers whose worth has risen as Marxism has bankrupted itself. Both Burke and De Tocqueville believed in the character of a people, that the French major in being French just as the Americans major in being American. There is no political God, only political legacies that people can extend and improve upon. West emphasized the need for improvements in the legacies; this is why she regarded herself more as a liberal than as a conservative. But she shared common ground with conservatives in that she treasured conservation and was willing to support a government that was 30% right as opposed to one that was 15% so. (I cite her figures.) In other words, she could live with the terribly flawed aspects of the positions she supported, recognizing the truth, however small, in other positions, and not pretending she had found her god.

There is no doubt that Rebecca West injured herself by throwing around the Communist label a little too freely. In the midst of fifties Cold War ferocity, she tended to label every political opponent a pinko, if not a Red. She did suffer an excess of virtue on the subject of anti-Communism. But as Doris Lessing insists, West was fundamentally right—not after the fact, but at the time when it mattered.

There remains a puzzle. How did West get it right so much sooner than others? Why did she never express even sympathy for the Soviets? For one thing, she did not confuse means and ends. She was not willing to overlook crimes in the Soviet regime because its ends (so people thought) were good. If the means were evil, the ends would be evil. To take away human rights and civil liberties was to take them away—they would not return on a better day.

West also believed in her own intellect and her assessment of human character. She could not brush off Emma Goldman the way Susan Sontag brushed off Czeslaw Milosz's *The Captive Mind*: "When it came out in 1953, I bought the book—a passionate account of the dishonesty and coerciveness of Communism, which troubled me but which I also regarded as an instrument of cold war propaganda, giving aid and comfort to McCarthyism." As Rebecca West would say, this is the logic of the status-conscious suburban housewife. Contrast Sontag's feeble apology with West's forthright ridicule of her Western colleagues who returned from brief trips to the Soviet Union with positive reports, or who palliated its problems. She observed that Goldman "is a Russian and speaks Russian as her native language. This equipment has been felt to be in the worst possible taste by other investigators of the Russian problem who lacked it." Emma Goldman spoke with enormous authority, and West paid her due respect. Milosz was no less an authority, and to have rejected him represents a shocking intellectual lapse.

But what gave West the wherewithal to accept Goldman's authority and the courage to stand by herself? Here biography helps. Her father, Charles Fairfield, was a brilliant, arch-conservative journalist, who by example taught his child to have faith in her own arguments and insight. In fact, she rejected many of his ideas, especially his anti-feminism, but what she absorbed was an unflinching intellectual rectitude. He was a man who was not afraid to go it alone, as her fictional portrait of him in *The Fountain Overflows* shows.[8]

But Charles Fairfield left his daughter a darker legacy, one which taught her to yearn for and yet to beware of the god that failed. He had been a brilliant man but an aloof father, with an Anglo-Irish aristocratic bearing, a contempt for his wife's lowly Scottish relations, an insatiable appetite for other women, and a reckless penchant for gambling away the rent money. West was only eight years old when he abandoned the family, going off to Africa in search of his fortune. He returned to die in Liverpool, virtually a pauper, when West was thirteen. She never saw him again after he left home. And she never stopped wanting him and blaming him for the hardship his desertion caused her, her mother, and her two older sisters, as her writing attests. Portraits of Charles Fairfield, of god-like male figures, abound in West's fiction, where they take the form of characters like the adulterous Edward Rowan, an Anglo-Irish politician who fails Laura Rowan and her mother in *The Birds Fall Down*.

The mad King Lear, arbitrary but grand, demanding that his daughters love him even as he destroys the possibility that their love can be freely granted him, haunted West's imagination. His story was both a familial and political metaphor—as she makes clear in her great study of politics and literature, *The Court and the Castle*, a book the distinguished critic John Wain ranked beside T.S. Eliot's finest prose. West hated Cordelia for not rebelling against her father as she had rebelled against Charles Fairfield. Yet West could no more forsake the idea of authority, traditionally invested in the male, than could Cordelia. Like Shakespeare, West was drawn to characters who had treason in the blood.

If *The Meaning of Treason* is West's profoundest study of "The God That Failed," that is because it fuses her biography with the main story of her book, "The Revolutionary," an account of the traitor, William Joyce (1906-1946), popularly known as Lord Haw. He grew up in a home rife with religious conflict but devoted to the British Empire. William's father, Michael, had made himself most unpopular in his native Ireland because of his pro-Unionist politics, and William adopted his father's allegiance—even enlisting in the British army before he was of age. There was something extraordinarily pure and touching about William's patriotism. During his brief army stint, his fellow recruits made sport of his earnestness by whistling "God Save the Queen," knowing that he would jump out of bed and stand to attention. Yet William knew there was something suspect in

---

8.   West treasured the story that her father had once engaged in a "wonderful" all-night debate with George Bernard Shaw.

his family history that cast doubt on his allegiance to the British Empire. He had been born in Brooklyn, New York, and feared that the British authorities would consider him an American citizen. It has never been proven whether or not William also knew that his father had become an American citizen, for Michael Joyce destroyed evidence of his American citizenship and claimed to be a British subject after he moved back to Ireland when William was still a young boy. William's treason trial would hinge on the issue of his citizenship. Did England have the right to try him after his American citizenship was established?

William's pro-British fervor revealed itself in a remarkable manner. At the age of sixteen he wrote to army officials expressing his desire to draw his sword for the Empire. His patriotism had been sharpened by a bitter awareness that he was in the despised minority in his native land; a love of the British was tantamount to treason. He was the product of mixed parentage (a Protestant father and Catholic mother), precocious, alienated from his native land, possessed of a sharp and eloquent tongue that often got him into fights—all qualities reminiscent of Rebecca West, but a West gone awry, so to speak, becoming involved with the British Fascists and indulging in a love for street fighting.

West's earliest memories of her father's conservatism, of reading writers such as Kipling, of revering the Royal Family (memories that came flooding back to her when she met the Queen during the war), equipped her to amplify Joyce's biography. She presented him as a sincere soul, an excellent tutor of young children, who perverted his own desire for distinction into an identification with totalitarianism, made necessary when England did not recognize his abilities, when its own Fascist leader, Oswald Mosley, failed to treat his deputy, William, with the respect William had worked so hard to earn. Joyce turns on England as if turning on a lover who has spurned him, and West imagines him leaving England at the beginning of the war to serve Hitler as a means of seeking a way to return triumphantly to London.

Exactly how William Joyce transformed himself from British patriot to traitor, from a Conservative to a Fascist, has never been fully explained. West succeeded in her biography of him because with psychological brilliance she extrapolated a convincing narrative, in which she equates the intensity of his desire to be accepted by the British with the intensity of his Fascism, a powerful new ideology that would restore an effete England to William Joyce's idealized and heroic version of it, a version England had failed to achieve during William's youth.

In West's biography, Joyce becomes Britain's insidious alter ego, invading British homes with an intimate, cocksure radio voice. She heard the plaintive tone of someone whom society had not taken unto itself. In Joyce's voice, she heard, no doubt, the sounds of her own sense of rejection. His passionate ambition was to exercise authority. West's passion had always been to thwart the authority others seemed to exercise over her. She compared the grief of Joyce's followers during his treason trial with the mourning of the early Christians—a particularly apposite analogy, since she found in Joyce a saintly devotion to his cause, even when he knew he was going to be executed.

For West family life determines the individual, and in her evocation of Joyce's background she remarks that he was being "strangled by the sheer tortuousness of his family destiny." For her, it is fated that this man's life should end on the gallows. His problem is that he wants to govern, not to be governed, West concludes, speaking again not only for Joyce but for herself and her vision of a humanity which is constantly straining against authority. Like West, Joyce was the "apple of his family's eye," and like her, he reacts to his family's confidence in his exceptional abilities with an extraordinary rebelliousness, as if his own genius is paradoxically inhibited by the family's claim on him. Joyce invested Fascism with an international character, she argues, so that Fascism sanctioned his betrayal of family and country in a way that other British Fascists, such as Mosley, could not abide.

Those passages in which Joyce's character melds with West's become apparent when she shifts to suppositions. She has him embarking for Germany: "One day his little feet twinkled up the area of his basement flat near Earl's Court. His eyes must have been dancing." Such passages are bereft of evidence but full of her utter identification with her subject, her ability to show what joy it must have been to Joyce to turn traitor. Her prose is infectious, making readers also speculate on what "must have been."

Rebecca calls William Joyce "the revolutionary," a term she uses to define one who both hates order and loves it, who will destroy so that he might create a superior order. It is here that West took her stand in the postwar world against revolution, reaffirming what she had said twenty years earlier about the Russian Revolution—that it was bound to restore the tyranny of tsardom. One cannot murder society in order to save it. That William Joyce is transformed into the quintessential Rebecca West character is revealed in a single sentence: "He was not going to be king." Every dynamic character in her fiction and nonfiction sooner or later is measured in terms of royalty. Joyce's kingly attributes suggest to West that he is a symbol of humanity, that he has it in him to want simultaneously to live and to die. Like one of Shakespeare's heroes, his struggle is tragic. His example marks an "end to mediocrity."

It is an empathetic portrait, yet West affirms the court's decision that William Joyce must hang. All of her later writing is an effort to reconcile herself to authority and to study how badly things go wrong when those like Joyce will not submit to be governed. Even though he was not a British subject, she thought it right that he should be tried as a traitor. She carefully threaded her way through the legal arguments, affirming the rightness of the principle that allegiance draws protection and protection draws allegiance. William Joyce, in other words, conducted himself as a British citizen, traveled abroad on a British passport, had a claim to be protected by British laws and the British government—and by the same token was liable to be tried by them.

The very lengths to which West goes to justify this conclusion, however, suggest that it was a near thing in her own mind, that her own sympathies and the court's judgment could have gone the other way; that is, a part of her also believed that the individual has a right to throw off allegiance, a matter the lawyers debated for days during Joyce's trial. West concedes at the end of *The Meaning of Treason* that there is a case for the traitor and that all men should have a drop of treason in their blood. Otherwise, how can the status quo be challenged, how can a nation avoid the fatal complacency that could lead to its demise? Thus West presents herself as a hanging judge, with qualms. No more than Joyce did she ever see herself as acceptable, an Establishment figure.

Rebecca West never visited Russia. She never went through a conversion experience with Communism. It never represented the rainbow or an eschatological hope. Her father brought history home to her when she was just a little girl. She had revolutionaries in her home for dinner. At table she heard their arguments and saw them for the word-spinning zealots they were, and she knew for the rest of her life that there are visions of better worlds that are not worth the price.

REBECCA WEST AND THE FBI

This article appeared in The New Criterion. I consider it as the third part of my study of her politics, which began with "The God that Failed" and continued with "Rebecca West's Politics."

On October 19, 1992, I wrote to the Federal Bureau of Investigation requesting under the Freedom of Information Act to see Rebecca West's file. I had made a similar request for Lillian Hellman's files, and after several months—with help from my congressman—I received hundreds of pages of reports on Hellman's activities.[1] She had belonged to several Communist Front organizations. She had been involved in labor union drives in California. She was an outspoken Leftist and was often called a Stalinist. Most dramatically, she had had an affair with John Melby, a foreign service officer she had met in the U.S. embassy in Moscow. Even after names had been blacked out, the file was a fund of information. It contained accounts from informants and interviews with Hellman friends and associates. This was raw data—though the word data is misleading, since it implies factual material, and FBI files are more like gossip sheets that have to be stringently checked. Errors abound, not merely about a subject's political opinions and affiliations, but about the basics of his or her life. Unlike *The New Yorker*, the FBI does not employ fact checkers for its files. Nevertheless, these files help to pin down dates, episodes, and scenes in a subject's life. No biographer should be without the FBI dossier of his or her subject—if such a file exists.

---

1. FOIA requests often take a long time to process. Federal agencies have been slow to comply with the law—partly because it is time consuming to retrieve files, black out names (for so-called national security reasons), and then photocopy the file contents. I was in a hurry when doing my Hellman biography, having been given only fifteen months to complete the book by my publisher, St. Martin's Press. And I had a feisty Detroit congressman, George Crockett, known for his fearless attacks on government secrecy.

I was sure there was a file on Rebecca West, although I was also certain it would look nothing like Lillian Hellman's. Although West often described herself as a socialist—certainly as late as the end of World War II she was voting Labor—she had never been a Communist or a fellow traveler. Even as the revolution was triumphing in Russia in 1917, West voiced skepticism about the Bolsheviks. She made a curious comment about them, one that sounds frivolous. She said they talked too much. In fact, she had heard them talking in her home, where her conservative father often brought revolutionists (as they were sometimes called then) for debates. He had a fondness for them because he had been educated by two Frenchmen who had been active in the Commune of 1871. He rejected their politics but not the dialectical habit of mind. His precocious and curious daughter, then between the ages of five and eight in 1898-1901, observed these big talkers and drew conclusions about Bolshevism that were confirmed as she matured. Her final word on the revolutionists can be found in her great novel, *The Birds Fall Down*. The revolutionists talk and talk, and what they reveal is a monstrous inhumanity, a dedication to the idea of revolution with a total disregard for the very people they claim to be liberating. Of course, the ancien regime fares no better in this novel. Indeed, the Czarist party shares with the Bolsheviks a loquacity that is orgiastic, frenzied and self-indulgent, for West believed that Bolshevism would use the same autocratic methods as the old guard.[2] The Revolutionists would simply build on the czarist bureaucracy and secret police, and the cult of the czar would be replaced by the cult of the Bolshevik leader. This is why she makes her novel's main character a double agent, serving both the revolutionists and the reactionaries.

West regarded the Russian Revolution as a colossal mistake. But when President Wilson and others in the West attempted to abort the Bolshevik advance—even sending troops to help the Whites in Russia—West objected. Each nation had a right to work out its own destiny, she wrote in a preface to Emma Goldman's book, *My Disillusionment in Russia* (1924). Rebecca West was a fervent anti-Communist, but she was no red baiter. Indeed, she deplored the deportation of Goldman from the United States, and West praised Goldman for speaking out against the Palmer raids which rounded up Reds and violated their civil liberties.[3] When Goldman came to England in 1924 to denounce Bolshevik tyranny and to solicit aid from the British Left for her anti-Bolshevik campaign,

---

2. The phrase "orgiastic loquacity" appears in an article West wrote for the London *Daily News*, August 9, 1917, which expresses her doubts about the Bolsheviks. The article is reprinted in Jane Marcus, ed., *The Young Rebecca* (Bloomington: Indiana University Press, 1982).

West staunchly supported her even as figures such as Bertrand Russell and H. G. Wells refused to sanction Goldman's all-out attack on the Soviet Union. West had nothing but scorn for liberals and other Leftists who would not criticize the Soviet Union because the British Conservative Party and reactionary elements also attacked what West insisted was not a union of soviet socialist republics, but in fact simply Soviet Russia. She predicted that the British Labor Party and the cause of socialism would be doomed if the British Left blinked at Soviet tyranny. When she was not attacked for being merely a fanatical anti-Communist, she was ignored. Of course, West was right, and she was—as far as I know—the first person in the West to get it right while maintaining a Leftist orientation.

West believed that the future—however difficult—belonged to republican governments. When Franco attacked the Spanish republic, she supported the republic even though that meant supporting Communists, who were organizing much of the resistance to fascism. She gave money to Ralph Bates, one of her colleagues at the periodical *Time and Tide,* so that he could speak on behalf of the Spanish republic in the United States. West did not attach her name to the lists of Communist Front organizations and members that agitated on behalf of the Spanish republic, but she included herself in a pamphlet filled with writers' statements backing the republic.

By the beginning of World War II, West's strong anti-Communism placed her in a precarious position among her Leftist friends, a fact that can easily be ascertained from the Epilogue to her masterpiece, *Black Lamb and Grey Falcon* (1941). Her main charge against the Left is that it had been more concerned with the moral purity of its principles than with the struggle to gain political power. Rather than dealing with the compromises that any ruling majority has to make, the Left—particularly the Labor Party—had preferred its role as a virtuous minority. Small wonder, then, that reactionary and fascist forces had filled the power vacuum. She had also lost a good deal of faith in the socialist promise, though it would take the anti-diluvian attitudes of the labor unions in the 1950s, and her disgust with the hysteria over McCarthyism, to smother her last tender feelings toward the Left.

West got into a good deal of trouble with a series of articles for the London *Sunday Times* in March 1953 (reprinted in *U.S. News and World Report*) for advancing a position that was far more concerned about Communist infiltration

---

3. Alexander Mitchell Palmer (1872-1936) was U.S. Attorney General from 1919-1921. At his direction, three thousand allegedly subversive aliens were arrested for deportation. Most were eventually released, with only about two hundred people actually being deported.

of Western governments and with the tyrannical policies of Communist regimes than with the relatively petty annoyance of Communist witchhunts. As she made clear in a series of biographical articles on Stalin in the London *Evening Standard*, Communism was not a political ideology; it was a criminal conspiracy that deserved to be investigated and rooted out of Western democracies.

So why should I think that Rebecca West had an FBI file? If there ever was a figure above suspicion as a subversive, it was certainly Rebecca West. But dossiers were assembled not just on Communists and fellow travelers. The FBI investigated all sorts of people in the public eye. More importantly, West had an impressive record of contacts with government agencies and offices. She could well have been an informant for the FBI or other agencies such as the CIA. She knew the CIA's first director, Allen Dulles, quite well. Her husband, Henry Andrews, knew Dulles from the 1920s and 1930s, when Dulles worked on Wall Street. West talked politics with Dulles; they met socially. They corresponded. During the 1930s West wrote a series of articles on the New Deal and got to know attorney general Francis Biddle—later one of the judges at the Nuremberg trials, when the two had an affair. Biddle told her that he regretted the shoddy hiring practices during the Roosevelt years; there had been a lot of log rolling—Communists hiring fellow Communists. Biddle told her things that he would never say publicly—things that no Democrat felt comfortable talking about, since the Republicans would surely use the open expression of such regrets to partisan advantage. Discussion of the extent of Communist infiltration of the New Deal was always skewed because, once again, liberals who knew about the infiltration did not want to abet the reactionaries who would use this knowledge to undermine New Deal policies. Instead, Truman initiated his own internal security programs that demanded such things as loyalty oaths.

In England, West had extraordinary contacts with the British Foreign Office. Her travels in Yugoslavia had made her a valuable source for the British government, and her husband's contacts in Germany and in Eastern Europe also made him a source of information about the German aircraft industry and on business enterprises in Nazi-occupied lands. Andrews had also been instrumental in spiriting many Jews out of Nazi Germany and had extensive contacts in the underground. West and Andrews knew the important figures in the London governments-in-exile during the war. The couple heard all the gossip about the intrigues involving Tito and the jostling for position in postwar Europe. Right after the war, West relied on her friendship with Theobald Mathew, who had been her attorney and advisor for years and was then Director of Public Prosecutions, to procure material for her coverage of the treason trials which resulted in her two great books of reportage, *The Meaning of Treason* and *A Train of Powder*. West loved law cases and government documents. Unlike many intellectuals, she understood modern administration and bureaucracy. She had a feel for what it was like to govern—not just a penchant for criticizing the governors. See, for example, her extraordinary book, *The Court and the Castle*, where she reveals her exquisite literary and political perceptions. She understands Kafka, for example, not only as a writer, but also as an official who worked for the Hapsburg bureaucracy.

So I was prepared to read a most unusual FBI file—one that would reveal a writer who had an inside knowledge of how modern governments dealt with security matters. Her profile would be nothing like those of most intellectuals who sign petitions and lend their names to causes out of a kind of sentimental Leftism, which still goes unexamined. I also knew something else. West had a direct pipeline into the House Committee on UnAmerican Activities (HUAC). She had an old American friend, Doris Stevens, whom West had first met in the 1920s when they shared a fervent devotion to feminism. Stevens later worked for the New Deal, then had been fired, and then had soured on the Roosevelts, angry that they had been co-opted by the Communists who had infiltrated the New Deal bureaucracy.

Stevens fed West information from HUAC files. She even interviewed Elizabeth Bentley, the so-called "Red Spy Queen," whom many on the Left ridiculed but whom Stevens and West believed. (Much of what seemed farfetched in Bentley's HUAC testimony has been corroborated in recent years). What is so impressive about West is that she did not merely read about Bentley but did her own investigative work. And she did not just read about HUAC, she looked at the way HUAC gathered its data—a far more scrupulous process than anyone could imagine from watching the buffoonery of congressman riding the anti-Communist bandwagon for self-serving purposes. HUAC made a poor impression in the media, but it had investigators doing serious research. It is shameful, of course, that HUAC often made a hash of that research—a point West conceded.

I made my request to the FBI in the autumn of 1992. I also wrote to other security agencies, such as the CIA and the NSA. I expected to wait up to a year for information. I bided my time because I had West's own extensive files and could track her political involvements through her correspondence and through the papers of her friends and associates. But I was stunned to learn that each agency claimed that it had nothing on West in its files. I surmised that the material had been destroyed sometime earlier or that an inadequate search had been made.

The FBI acknowledged my FOIA request on November 12, 1992, and I never heard from the agency again—that is until August 3, 1997—almost five years after my request and nearly two years after I had completed my biography of West. Her file arrived at my Baruch College office. Names had been blacked out and pages were missing, probably for any of the following reasons: an Executive order had established that this material be kept secret; revealing certain material would interfere with enforcement proceedings; disclosing the contents would invade privacy; confidential sources would be disclosed; techniques and procedures of law enforcement agencies would be revealed and thus risk circumvention of the law; the life or physical safety of individuals might be endangered.

Even with these exemptions, I got sixteen pages—a small file but a revealing one, nevertheless, about both Rebecca West and the FBI. The first page is a memorandum (August 22, 1955) from Mr. M. A. Jones to Mr. Nichols providing a capsule biography of the subject taken—as it often is in FBI files—from a standard reference book that contains significant errors. In this case, the mistake is the statement that West was born in Scotland. In fact, she was born in London, although she received much of her education in Edinburgh. The third sentence identifies her as an anti-Communist. The next sentence (bingo!) reports that she has furnished information to an FBI Liaison Representative (name blacked out) in England "on a number of occasions." It is noted that she wrote to the FBI requesting information about the Rosenberg and Fuchs spy cases, about which she later wrote articles.[4] Mr. Jones cites a memorandum of May 1953 that his colleague Mr. Jones wrote to Clyde Tolson (J. Edgar Hoover's right-hand man) observing that West had written articles defending "McCarthyism." These were the *U. S. News and World Report* articles that got West into trouble with American liberals. She would have vehemently denied that she was defending McCarthyism; rather, her articles treated him as a sideshow—not a menace to the Republic.

Mr. Jones reports that West has stated she knows John Foster Dulles "very well." I never found any support for that claim—if she made it. He also refers to Mr. Nichols's memo from 1951 about West's "vociferous" writing about traitors. Her travels in Yugoslavia, her reports on the Nuremberg trials, and her interest in the Hiss case are all duly noted in this "synopsis" Mr. Jones provides for Mr. Nichols. The FBI had not only followed West's travels and her writing, it took

---

4.   In fact, as the FBI file later reveals, in December 1952, West wrote directly to J. Edgar Hoover about the Rosenbergs. She was not, however, given information because the case was then being appealed.

note of her contacts with Europeans who "came to her with information." She had conveyed to Clyde Tolson (whether in person, in writing, or indirectly is not clear because the memo is blacked out at this point) the names of important Soviet agents in America. The FBI had investigated her source, a TASS representative, but Mr. Jones does not comment on the accuracy of her statement. He also acknowledges her article, "Opera in Greenville," concerning a lynching in Greenville, South Carolina, which contained, he says, "an unfavorable reference to the Bureau." (She had criticized the FBI's possibly "illegitimate methods" of obtaining statements from witnesses.)

Much of the material in West's dossier is repetitive—a characteristic of many FBI files. Subsequent pages fill in details about her education and publication history. The FBI took keen interest in how she phrased her anti-Communist position. For instance, it remarked that one of her *Sunday Times* articles concluded that the printed record of Congressional investigations of Communism "shows no more inquisitiveness at work…than the situation would have provoked in any society not manifestly insane." She had also called the word "witch-hunting" the "careless repetition of an impudent piece of Communist propaganda." Although such statements outraged many liberals, the FBI file points out that the *U.S. News and World Report* reprint of the *Sunday Times* articles had provoked a phenomenal reaction: "All issues of the magazine had been sold out and…the magazine's mail had been unprecedented—most letters upholding West's view."

Mr. Jones charted the trajectory of West's involvement in Yugoslavia and how she had been accused of allying herself with the country's right-wing parties and with a banker husband who had financial interests in Eastern Europe. West denied these allegations, Mr. Jones points out. Her husband had no property or investments in Yugoslavia or in businesses dealing with that country, and she was not a reactionary—although she added in a preface to David Martin's book, *Ally Betrayed* (an account of how the West had abandoned General Mihailovic for Marshall Tito):

> I am a socialist. But I have to admit that in the last few years the Left Wing has shown itself just about as good a custodian of the sacred principle of Liberty, Fraternity, and Equality, as the watchdog who was found holding a lamp in his mouth for the burglar who was cracking the safe.

This criticism, voiced in 1947, would be confirmed for West straightaway in the credulous position that the Left adopted in the Hiss/Chambers case. She would call it the Dreyfus case in reverse: whereas Dreyfus had been the victim of those who immediately presumed him guilty, Hiss became the darling of liberals who automatically assumed and indeed demanded that Hiss be declared innocent. Mr. Jones comments that the media was beginning to slot West into a reactionary niche. He quotes a *New York Times* article (January 18, 1948), which observes that West adored Yugoslavia "and its vivid inhabitants from what one may call the right wing side of the fence politically."

In October 1950, the FBI's Baltimore office had further confirmation of West's impressive sources on the subject of Communist infiltration of Western governments. In an FBI interview with Whittaker Chambers, he revealed that he had been told (the name of his informant is blacked out) that before the Hiss case broke in America, a young Czech woman had told West that Hiss was a Russian spy. The FBI then interviewed the woman, who corroborated what she had told West and what Chambers had passed on to the FBI. Apparently West had not gone to the FBI or to British security, concluding after a discussion with her husband that "she had no business getting involved in the controversy" Mr. Jones reports. The FBI, working through its legal attaché in London, took steps to set up an interview with West. Later pages in her file reveal that on August 17, 1951, she provided the FBI with substantial background information on Communist activities.

The London interview was evidently a dousy. The legal attaché had been prepped for the interview with the cautionary observation that West was "irritable and suspicious" but also "extremely conscientious, intelligent, sincere and needing to be treated with patience and candor." West revealed that a TASS representative had approached her while she was covering the Progressive Party presidential convention in Philadelphia in 1948. She not only relayed what he said but added much more, though how valuable it was to the FBI is uncertain, since some of it was judged "largely nonspecific." But that phrase refers to material or to persons who are blacked out. West may have been a little cagey, for her file notes:

> She advised she preferred furnishing the information to American authorities since she had little confidence in British Intelligence and the Director of Public Prosecutions in London. She previously had furnished the Public Prosecutor information concerning Communists in Government, but no action had been taken.

West was re-interviewed in September 1951 and on other occasions, Mr. Jones reports.

How reliable was West's information? The FBI considered the question carefully. She was unsure about details. For example, she could give only a phonetic spelling for the TASS representative she had interviewed. It was hard getting a complete picture from her. Rebecca West was one of the great talkers of the western world, but on the subject of Communism she managed to bore even the FBI! Her remarks are characterized as "rather tedious." It is also eyebrow raising for a member of the Bureau to call her "very sensitive and imaginative and certainly fanatic on the subject of Communism." The ultimate conclusion, however, was that "she undoubtedly had seen a person (Tass representative) who in all probability had furnished her information concerning Soviet spies and Communists."

West's confidence in the FBI—as opposed to the British security services—never wavered. For example, she alerted the FBI that in February 1953 she had seen the galleys of William Allen Jowitt's book, *The Strange Case of Alger Hiss*, and that the book took an unfavorable attitude toward the FBI. She was so incensed after a dinner with Charlie Chaplin, in which he brazenly broadcast his Communist views, that she had contacted the Bureau, calling Chaplin "crazy." He was an ex-lover, whom she had seen in Rome while trying to write a screenplay for Roberto Rosselini, whom she also found to be infected with Communist enthusiasm. A blacked out section covering events during this period has an asterisk after it with the comment that at least some of West's allegations could not be substantiated.

It is impossible to tell, in the end, how good an informant Rebecca West made. At least three pages of her file have been removed. What is striking is that she apparently never mentioned any of her liberal American friends—anyone who might fall under the FBI's suspicion. She often had arguments with American liberals who thought she had a blind spot about McCarthyism, and she got angry at people like Arthur Schlesinger who tried to get her to reconsider her view that McCarthy had done no significant damage to American institutions or to the political climate.

West, in truth, was far more concerned with how the FBI regarded her than she was worried about the criticism of liberals. In November 1953, for example, she wrote a letter to the Bureau explaining that her article on the dangers of radioactivity should not be taken as some kind of "anti-H-bomb or unilateral disarmament campaign" piece. What the Bureau called her active imagination is revealed in this letter (which is part of her FBI file) in which she fears that "some form of Intelligence might be wrinkling its brows" over her article. Near the end of her file is her acknowledgement of J. Edgar Hoover's letter congratulating her on the honor of having been named Dame of the British Empire. Seeing her letter gave me a shock—not so much for what it says (the letter is in character), but because Hoover's letter is not in West's papers, and I am sure she treasured it. Her words to Hoover sound an entirely conservative note, but then on March 7, 1959—when she wrote the letter—she did believe that the West was engaged in an apocalyptic struggle with Communism. She had come to believe that without law there can be no order or liberty. "It was most kind of you to send me your congratulations on my Damehood or Dameship, I haven't myself yet grasped what it should be called," West wrote Hoover. "I am proud of my honour, and proud too that the F.B.I. should have sent me their good wishes. Long may they live to establish law and order!"

J. Edgar Hoover has become, of course, the great bugbear of American liberals, and West's letter will no doubt make the Left wince. She could be more fanatical on the subject of anti-Communism than the FBI—but then she thought that her side (the Left) had let her down, and she was badly in need of allies and of acknowledgement, both of which the FBI gave her. Her file confirms a side of her my biography of her also shows: she felt (I think justifiably) isolated. Her outspoken anti-Communism got her tagged not only as a conservative or a reactionary; it also hurt her in the literary world, where her magnificent grasp of political reality and of political institutions is still shunned.

West reached a turning point, I believe, when Stalin made his pact with Hitler. She noted that many of the founders of the Bolshevik Party were Jewish—not to mention Karl Marx himself. That Stalin could strike a deal with the man responsible for the Holocaust (and she knew about the concentration camps long before Western governments acknowledged their existence) proved that Soviet Russia was nothing more than a criminal regime. She was revolted at the way so much of the Left ignored Stalin's culpability. I think it is her loathing for this tyranny that overrode any consideration she might otherwise have given to the evils of McCarthyism.

With evils as massive as Communism and Fascism, West put no stock in Leftist sentiments as a way to counteract tyranny. Institutions like the FBI were essential. In a little known, brief essay, she explained how her political attitudes had evolved. She had grown up in a world that prized rebellion, and she had been a rebel. She supposed that human beings were naturally good and that the law was a cumbersome instrument that dealt harshly with people. Law would lose its sway when the revolution brought an end to poverty and evil. Two wars, the concentration camps, and totalitarian government convinced her that the good in people was not merely a quality to be brought out. It had to be created by an effort of love and a submission to the "Rule of Law."[5]

West's letter to Hoover acknowledges his authority. Too often, in her view, dissent had turned into an attack on the idea of authority itself. Her letter is, if you will, a kind of submission. West was not surrendering her freedom to criticize Hoover and government institutions, but she was recognizing his rightful role in upholding the law. At the same time, she recognized not merely the role of the dissenter but of the traitor, arguing in *The Meaning of Treason*, that it was good for individuals to have a drop of treason in their blood. Society did not change, and it could not improve, without challenges to authority.

The FBI welcomed and yet was understandably wary of Rebecca West's contributions to its anti-Communist investigations. She had an incandescent mind. Her niece has said that if she ever came back it would be as a firework. There is a memo from an FBI official to Hoover, forwarding that letter West wrote expressing her concern that her article on the hydrogen bomb and the dangers of radioactivity would be taken the wrong way by the FBI. The memo notes that "apparently Miss West envisions some chain reaction to her article among intelligence circles...." The official's metaphor of the chain reaction is appropriate. West thought of herself as producing fissionable material, nuclear reactions that could set off political explosions. I sympathize with those FBI agents attempting to track dialectical arguments. As her recently released FBI file suggests, the repercussions of Rebecca West's protean imagination have yet to be investigated.

5.   Edward P. Morgan, ed., *This I Believe* (New York: Simon and Schuster, 1952).

APPENDIX

The Rebecca West-Doris Stevens File 1947-1959

The correspondence between Rebecca West and Doris Stevens reveals the post World War II climate in which West's anti-Communism flourished. She often felt besieged, and her feelings of persecution propelled her toward the FBI. The letters also reveal the way she believed that Communists and fellow travelers worked to undermine and to discredit the work of anti-Communists, and her determination to fight back.

> [October 26, 1947] I was falsely charged with slandering one of the Labour M.P.'s.... They thought they had got enough on me to shut me up, then started a campaign against me in the New Statesman. The second stage of the campaign was a letter from an American living in London called Robert Solo—accusing me of anti-Semitism. Now, I have a recollection of seeing his name in connection with the New Masses or some other Communist paper. Can you help me on this?

> [August 29, 1948] [Don Hollenbeck, in CBS LOOKS AT THE PRESS] blasted me in an incredible script—concentrating on the fact that I was old, fat, and ugly, and owned Jersey cows—on my Wallace Convention articles. Then, a fortnight later, came back to it. Then his whim was to piece together my Evening Standard articles in such a way that he could frame a piece together informing the United States that I had written articles for England which were anti-American and anti-Negro...Now, the significant thing about this is that the London Daily Worker had started to blast me as anti-Negro; and my leak in the Communist camp tells me that the London Daily Worker was busily working on my material.... Can we put the heat on him [Hollenbeck]?

[December 29, 1948] I imagine that the Hiss and Chambers case as it develops gives you something that you feel worth while—at least people are having their eyes open.... There is a complete misapprehension as to what has happened, and I have found it uphill work convincing people there is something which is going on....

[June 7, 1950] Thank you for that armful of reports from the Un-American Activities Committee.

[August 21, 1950, DS to RW] Ben Mandel of the Un-Am.Actc.Cttee staff wrote me he had "solved the difficulty of putting me on the list for an "extra copy of everything" which I could send to you.

[October 25, 1950, DS to RW] My memo to you [about Elizabeth Bentley] is based on notes taken down from her miles of talk, boiled down and read back to her and approved by her....

[January 14, 1951] Did I write you about the Elizabeth B stuff? Because it was superb.... I have done a review of Alistair Cooke's iniquitous book on the Hiss case in Time & Tide (which I enclose) and have written a much longer review for the University of Chicago Law Review. Dick Crossman (the Labour M.P.) is trying to fix up a dialogue on it between us on the radio, but you know how strong Communist influence is there. I have tried to do what I can for the Toledano & Lasky book, which has had a poor show.... I have used those Committee reports well...I am not mentioning Elizabeth B.'s book in my chapter because her book will be out long before mine, but I will boost her book good and hard, and hope to find an opportunity for doing so quite soon.

[April 26, 1951] I believe Chambers—tho' I don't like or trust him—why wasn't Hiss sentenced for espionage instead of perjury—why was Chambers protecting him and others involved, in the State Department.... I couldn't help thinking that Chambers and others were in love with Hiss and C was afraid that the story would come out—Jan says I have a low mind—well, I have, so what?

[May 25, 1951] I am writing six articles of a popular kind for Everybody Weekly—the Canadian Spy Ring, the Hiss case, the Atom Scientists, the Rosenbergs—not because I want to, I can ill spare the time, but nobody else is telling the story.

[June 9, 1951] About the F.O. men: Burgess, the Far Eastern boy, came into my life when I was fighting a lone hand for Mihailovitch during the war. A MOST SUSPICIOUS CHARACTER in the F.O. introduced himself to Henry and tried to lay the foundations of a beautiful friendship, but I would have none of it. For one thing because I knew he was in a set of Communist writers and painters of the rich pansy or promiscuous set. I forgot him…I forgot him so completely that there was a funny scene on Election Night when we went to Lord Kemsley's Party and friends asked us to have supper at their table. I sat next this young man, who was not a friend of my friends but of some friends of theirs to whom they were united solely by business interests. He recalled that we had met, and presently I remembered that he had been one of the anti Mihailovitch boys, and coldly asked him if he was a friend of the MOST SUSPICIOUS CHARACTER and another one. When he said, "Yes," with a sweet smile, I turned my back on him. Afterwards, Henry (who had missed all this) told me it was Burgess…. I have always felt that there is a Communist very high up in the Foreign Office…. I have tried for years to get Orme Sargent, the former head of the F.O., to take this seriously but he wasn't a Communist but was a damned fool.

[Sept 22, 1951] <u>What</u> a story! I cannot think how anybody could have doubted Elizabeth Bentley's story for a moment, there was so much collaborative material. It shows the strength of the movement to bewitch the press.

[December 8, 1951] Elizabeth B is a queer fish, because she does not know what it is all about, even yet…. I admire her character and I am glad she acted as she did, but she does not seem to me a true anti-Communist. She would have stayed right there if Mr Golos had not passed on to the next world.

[Feb 5, 1952]…it is absurd when a known anti-Communist like Graham Greene is denied a visa, it is worse when a scientist like Michael Polanyi, who is one of the most steadying anti-Red influences on young communists, and who has immense prestige owing to his unique talents, is prevented from entering America. I know Polanyi, and I know he is all right. If you can get me the American view of him I should be most grateful. I say it solemnly—this is a disaster.

[Feb 6, 1952] Francis Biddle is certainly not a Communist or a fellow-traveller, but a damned fool, and he feels uncomfortable about the number of people he cleared when he was A.G. That is all I should say there was to it in his case, and anyways he cannot put a foot right just now.

[April 21, 1952] I have reviewed Chambers' book for the Atlantic Monthly. A Queer, queer creature, and one of those that never quite get the poison out of their blood. He talks a great deal of nonsense about the Communists, talking about the Party as if it were the early Church instead of the vast pork-barrel that it is.

[August 28, 1952] In the beginning of a most mysterious political campaign! Practically no faction of either party is happy about what is going on. Only the commies & their followers are pleased. Everything is so inter-meshed now, the

Kremlin might well be pushing the buttons. You have to be here to believe it. Otherwise, it's past belief.

[November 10, 1952, DS to RW] The only disappointment I had about your review of Lattimore's book was that you had to be so prudent. I understand why, libel laws being what they are.

[Feb 13, 1953]...the Sunday Times has asked me to write two long, really long, hallelujah, articles on the Hiss Case and its aftermath. 3,500 words each. I intend to do a lot about the infiltration of the Civil Service.... I am so damned mad that my Tito Speaks review was killed. And so damned mad that Margaret Rhondda has been got hold of by a Foreign Office pork-barrel-pink (Charles Peake) and turned pro-Tito. But this opportunity partly consoles me.

[March 30, 1953]...I think that Senator McCarthy has put his foot in it badly, over the fleet of ships business, and I wish to God he had handled the Bohlen business differently. I wish he wasn't so much associated with the Investigation business, for which you and Jon among other people have done far more. My references to him may not please you, but not for one minute do I let go of the principle of the thing.

[March 31, 1953] We are getting shoals of letters over my Sunday Times articles—all terrified of McCarthy, whom they think of as an ogre that eats professors for breakfast.

[August 21, 1953] I am being attacked right left and centre all the time, and feel much refreshed by such letters as I had the other day from Bertrand D. Wolfe, which I felt an honour...I did get a horrid feeling when I heard that there was a whispering campaign in London that I had gone mad, and that my articles on Communism were part of my madness. But I knew I was letting myself in for trouble when I decided to write these articles, and it is even a consolation to think that there cannot be many more years for people to do me hard, since really this policy of appeasement is so shameful. I think the reason for it here is that we are too tired by two wars, we are as France was after the First World War—but I wish to God we would be honest and say so, and not pretend that we were doing the right thing and wouldn't do differently if we could.

[November 23, 1953] Normally I make about a hundred and twenty pounds a month from newspaper articles and weekly articles and reviews. My income during this period [since March] has been <u>nil</u>. (I don't mean this is the whole of my income, this is my British journalistic income, my bread and butter, on which the rest is kept for larger expenditures). Furthermore, the people in the Sunday Times who loathed my articles have been spreading the story that I am insane, asylum insane, and am not safe to employ or know. I shall weather this. But it is unpleasant, though as I knew I was in for some unpleasantness when I wrote those articles it is at least not a shock.... The real tragedy of the situation is Eisenhower's fatal weakness. They thought nothing of him at Columbia University, you know, because he was such an eternal compromiser. He never stood by anything or anybody, he fiddled. I don't think he holds aloof from Brownell and the anti-Communist campaign because he disapproves of what they do but because he can't bear to be attacked by the Democrats, which is a damn silly attitude for a Republican President. He should have talked out the situation relating to the scandal of the Democratic administration's infiltration long ago, and given his Party a line. He should have controlled Senator McCarthy; he shouldn't do this obliquely by letting the War Department give the impression that there was nothing of Communist infiltration in the Signals Corps, when the fact that there was is written into the Rosenberg trails. I fear he is a bad President, and that may be very awkward for us....

[July 1, 1955] The horrid Communism of people like these Oxford dons. It is all a mixture of greed and snobbery trying to keep its position in case of a revolution.

[April 3, 1959] [Kitty] then added to her charm by telling me lightheartedly that yes, she had once been a Communist. "We all were," she said happily because of certain events. Now, I have asked her again and again if Anthony was ever a Communist, explaining to her that I wanted the knowledge in order not to hurt but to protect Anthony. She has denied any connection with the Party. I didn't quite believe her, and I threw myself on the mercy of the American authorities, with the aid of Norris, and told them that it might be that Anthony had been a Communist but that it would be a terrible thing if he were deported, and his naturalisation revoked, for his only chance of happiness lay in the States, and if he were sent back here he would certainly blame me and I would be terrified for my peace, if not for my life....

[October 16, 1953 DS to RW] As to Anthony: As everybody knows, practically all normal children go through a period of resentment against their parents when they are getting up their courage to leave home. When I stop to think about it, what is communism but an attempt to institutionalize that otherwise transitory emotion? Marx saw his problem as breaking the continuity of family and community attitudes. Only thus could the world get a new start. How important this became we all know from Communist children denouncing parents, etc.... Which leads me to my point: Isn't it possible that Anthony's lack of tenderness toward you comes...from his being overtaken by the party at a critical point so that as long as he remains under Communist influence he'll be perpetually in that phase just as a wooly mammoth overtaken by a glacier in Siberia remains fresh, tender and edible after twenty thousand years?

REPORTING NUREMBERG
MARTHA GELLHORN,
JANET FLANNER, REBECCA
WEST,
AND THE NUREMBERG
TRIALS

This article first appeared in The New Criterion. It is another of my efforts to show how truly original West was, even in this distinguished league of female correspondents.

Only Martha Gellhorn, among these three journalists, became a war correspondent. In part, this turn of events was the product of timing. Gellhorn was born in 1908. As a writer, she was approaching her prime during the Spanish Civil War, and her experiences there equipped her magnificently for her role in reporting World War II (her work is recognized in the Library of America collection of World War II journalism). Also, the idea of the engaged writer, pioneered by Stephen Crane and apotheosized by Ernest Hemingway, had an enormous influence on Gellhorn, growing up in St. Louis and yearning by her twelfth year for adventure abroad. Janet Flanner and Rebecca West (both born in 1892) came a generation earlier and emerged from the Gilded Age and the Edwardian era, periods which saw figures such as Mark Twain and H. G. Wells enlivening English prose and making it a supple weapon against the status quo.

The lives and writings of these three women converged and diverged in fascinating and instructive ways. Gellhorn knew Flanner and West; indeed, Gellhorn became (briefly) H. G. Wells's mistress, a fact that Rebecca West (who earlier had a ten-year affair with Wells) never knew. Gellhorn and West visited Germany frequently in the early 1930s, witnessed the rise of Nazism, become Germanophobes, and realized immediately that the world was headed for another war. All three women were published in *The New Yorker*, although Gellhorn's regular beat was *Collier's* magazine. All three women were Francophiles, Flanner spending nearly her whole writing life reporting on France for *The New Yorker*, and much of West's postwar reporting on treason trials appeared at the instigation of the magazine's editor, Harold Ross. In fact, Ross assigned West to cover the Nuremberg trials when he found they did not suit Flanner—who admitted (somewhat enviously) that West's reporting had been better than her own. Curiously, all three women were at Nuremberg and yet did not meet. They shared much as journalists, yet their reports on Nuremberg reflect different tempers and styles—Gellhorn the war correspondent concerned with the unfolding of events; Flanner, the analyst, exploring subtleties of character and nuances of atmosphere; West, the dramatist of treason trials, probing the ethical implications of human behavior.

For all three, one disturbing figure dominates Nuremberg: Herman Goering. Of the twenty-one defendants, he is the only one to open his mind and to cast its contents defiantly into the courtroom. His fellow defendants and their lawyers build their cases around him, Flanner observes. He is their bastion, a star, sometimes resembling an "aging, fat tenor," sometimes a "middle-aged, fleshy contralto."[1] Goering makes an aria out of the sellout of Europe, reminding his accusers of how they had to let it go, country by country. Goering exudes power; he does not defer everything to the Fuhrer. The Anschluss and Munich were Goering's doing; Danzig was the Fuhrer's. In twenty-one hours of testimony Goering gives a guided tour of what Flanner calls the "most cynical military period in Europe's history." Economics, diplomacy, war—Goering covers it all, with savage humor, little remorse, and no conscience. Noting how he punctuates his bravura performance with his large white waving hands, Flanner has no trouble imagining how he has torn apart millions of lives.

Goering's triumph would be less shattering if he had not also made Robert Jackson, Justice of the United States Supreme Court, one of his victims. Jackson had opened the trials with a noble, stirring defense of the Nuremberg idea: that there were crimes against humanity that could not go unpunished. But face-to-face with evil, Jackson lacks the ideas and the personality to match Goering's. The Reichsmarschall outmaneuvers the Justice, exhibiting a keener memory and a firmer grasp of Nazi and European history. A dismayed Flanner thinks the

---

1. Flanner's writing on Nuremberg appears in *Janet Flanner's World: Uncollected Writings 1932-1975* (New York: Harcourt Brace Jovanovich, 1979).

shrewd Goering absolutely diabolical in "drawing on American and English history for familiar paradoxes and damaging precedents." Even the best legal minds are flummoxed by his "fantastic and formidable personality." Physically, Jackson seems to shrink in Goering's presence; his habit of unbuttoning his coat, whisking it back over his hips, and sticking his hands in his back pockets remind Flanner of a country lawyer out of his depth.

A relieved Flanner watches the more skillful British Chief Prosecutor, Sir David Maxwell Fyfe, corner Goering. getting him to acknowledge the "difference between the glorified Nazi plan and the ghastly human results." Even better, the blunt Russian chief prosecutor, Roman Andreyevich Rudenko, handles Goering roughly, reminding him and the court of the Nazis' atrocities. But Flanner's conclusion is troubling: not much has been done really to establish the principles of Nuremberg. Rather, it is the German obsession with record-keeping that has allowed the Allies to convict the Nazis; they have incriminated themselves with their own documents.

Martha Gellhorn comes to Nuremberg a battle-hardened veteran. She has traveled with Allied soldiers of many nationalities who have pushed the Nazis up and out of Italy. She has seen the Normandy beaches shortly after the invasion. She has been to Dachau. She knows Nuremberg is right. For her, the Reichsmarschall is a has-been actor, described in the past tense: "Goering's terrible mouth wore a smile that was not a smile, but only a habit the lips had taken."[2] Goering's puffy performances rebound off Gellhorn as though she is granite. All the defendants are similarly diminished: "These twenty-one men, these nothings, these industrious and once-confident monsters were the last left alive of that small gang which had ruled Germany." Flanner's awesome Goering and his lot are dispatched, a pathetic heap. Except for his "terrible mouth," Gellhorn gives him no dominating characteristic—indeed she does not describe him at all.

Gellhorn sees a courtroom that a reader of Flanner could not imagine:

> Everything about the trial at Nuremberg was unique in history; everything happened for the first time. Everyone present seemed to know that history was being made; everyone seemed to feel that responsibility and find it heavy.

The absoluteness of Gellhorn's prose situates her on solid ground immeasurably distant from Flanner's tentative terrain The courtroom has a grandeur because it

---

2.   Gellhorn's writing on Nuremberg appears in *The Face of War* (New York: Atlantic Monthly Press, 1988).

is re-establishing the rule of law. Lord Justice Geoffrey Lawrence, president of the tribunal, speaks in a "slow, careful, and immensely quiet voice." Listening to him "reading without haste or passion…You felt the dignity and modesty of the man…. That voice was speaking for history," Gellhorn concludes. She easily slips into the second person, having no doubt that she feels what you would feel had you been there. Listening to Lord Justice Lawrence, you feel, Gellhorn implies, that the verdict of the court is virtually divine.

Gellhorn has no illusions that Nuremberg will make the world a better place. But it is the least that can be done. By the end of her report, Goering is an evil memory, the flaws and failures in the court proceedings are not even mentioned. What is important is that "four nations could work patiently together to brand evil and reaffirm the power and the goodness of honest law."

Rebecca West arrives in Nuremberg later than Flanner and Gellhorn. The trials are almost over. But she is an old hand at trials and will soon publish a book about them, *The Meaning of Treason*. Goering fascinates her. She too fastens on his mouth, on his "wide and woodenish lips."[3] She refers to his "smiling wooden mask." He is a bit of a fake that Gellhorn portrays but also considerably like the demonic force that Flanner pictures. He is a man of enormous appetite. West imagines:

> If he were given the chance, he would walk out of the Palace of Justice, take over Germany again, and turn it into a stage for the enactment of his governing fantasy, which is so strong that it fills the air around him with its images, so madly private that those images are beyond the power of those who see them to interpret them.

West also found something soft and peculiarly sexual about Goering—not homosexual, she added, "but when his humor is good, he recalls the madam of a brothel."

Throughout her Nuremberg report, West combines the psychological and political, giving each their due, and consequently she provides a rounded, complex reading of history. Like so many of the characters she portrays in her fiction and nonfiction, the Reichsmarschall is full of life and death. When he balloons in importance, she brings him back to earth. The sense of corruption, of everything

---

3.   Rebecca West, "Extraordinary Exile," *The New Yorker*, September 7, 1946. A much revised version of West's Nuremberg report appears in *A Train of Powder* (New York: Viking, 1955). I am quoting from *The New Yorker* article.

for sale, pulses with life in West's portrait. Goering makes a whore of history, and he has the figure, the dress, and the makeup for it:

> He wears either a German air-force uniform or a light beach suit in the worst of playful taste, and both hang loosely on him, giving him an air of pregnancy. He has thick brown young hair, the coarse, bright skin of an actor who has used grease paint for decades, and the preternaturally deep wrinkles of the drug addict; it adds up to something like the head of a ventriloquist's dummy.

West had a fabled knack for taking her subject's measure, for using biography to suggest social, sexual, psychological, and historical significance. Goering had met his match.

In *A Train of Powder*, which contains West's most important writing on post-war Germany, she transforms Nuremberg into the story of the German imagination, of its penchant for fairy tales and overbuilding, its Wagnerian dreams of grandeur, which contribute to the excesses of Nazism. In a Schloss, an old nineteenth-century mansion she finds a metaphor for this Germanic need to overproduce and to dominate. She expects the mansion's greenhouse to be like the English variety, "a desert place of shabby and unpainted staging, meagerly set out with a diminished store of seed boxes. Instead, it is neat, clean, full of plants, and perfect, flourishing in the hands of a crippled gardener's single-minded devotion prophetic of Germany's rebirth. The scene at the Nuremberg Schloss becomes West's own tribute to and warning about the self-dedication and dynamism of German culture, which she regards as a great force for both good and evil. She knows that Germans are perfectly capable of transforming their fairy tale desire for a happy ending into "Lear's kingdom of loss."

Like Gellhorn, West believes in Nuremberg's importance, but like Flanner, she cannot gainsay its failures. Although she believes that the trials make a profound statement, settling once and for all that crimes against humanity should be punished, the Nuremberg judges, she realizes, are compromised. The Allies have committed some of the indictable crimes, such as unrestricted submarine warfare. American and British judicial procedures baffle the German attorneys, who do not understand the role of cross-examination, because in Germany judges take an active role in questioning witnesses. "The trouble about Nuremberg" she writes in *A Train of Powder*, was that it was so manifestly a part of life as it is lived; the trial had not sufficiently detached itself from the "oddity of the world."

The brilliance of West's report on Nuremberg is that it so manifestly evokes the trials as they were conducted, but it does not detach itself from the oddity of the world, the politics of war, or the desire to make sense of it all. Unlike Flanner,

West does not retreat from the trial's problematic denouement; unlike, Gellhorn, she does not evade its ambiguities.

It is to West that writers return, with the fiftieth anniversary of the Nuremberg trials just past, and with the conflicts in the former Yugoslavia still unresolved. Whether it is Telford Taylor in *The Anatomy of the Nuremberg Trials* (1993) invoking *A Train of Powder*, or Robert Kaplan in *Balkan Ghosts* (1993) producing a scaled down version of her great epic, *Black Lamb and Grey Falcon* (1941), West has become a touchstone.

In my biography I call her career a saga of the century. As a novelist, biographer, literary critic, journalist, early feminist, and staunch anti-Communist, she writes about the shaping of contemporary consciousness, seen through the eyes of an Englishwoman—as she refers to herself in *Black Lamb and Grey Falcon*. It is, paradoxically, this very personal and yet historical voice that makes her unique but still relevant. She is not afraid to speak for herself and for history. Few writers would approach Yugoslavia, Nuremberg—or any other subject for that matter—daring to assume such authority.

What would West have to say today as the world once again tries to bring war criminals to justice? The West is just as compromised now as it was at the end of the World War II. She had spent the 1930s arguing against appeasers and isolationists, and then watched her beloved Yugoslavia be torn apart and her own country bombed. She would not now abide standing aside because the various peoples of Yugoslavia have been in conflict since the fourteenth century. She loved the polyglot, multicultural confluences of Yugoslavia and would have rejected any effort to partition the country into ethnic enclaves.

Today, West might well quote that famous passage from *Black Lamb and Grey Falcon*:

> Only part of us is sane: only part of us loves pleasure and the longer day of happiness, wants to live to our nineties and die in peace, in a house that we have built, that shall shelter those who come after us. The other half of us is nearly mad…This fight can be observed constantly in our personal lives.

West had a gift for bringing history home, for showing how it functions in our daily lives. In her eyes, humanity's self-destructiveness does not make everyone Nazis, but in the passage above she explains how it is that a Goering could triumph. He could speak to that mad, war-like self that has made of Yugoslavia a holocaust. West had examined her darker nature and ours. She understood that both individuals and civilizations had constantly to strive for sanity and that

Nuremberg was part of that struggle. It was not only a trial of the accused but a trial of those who witnessed it. Now, as then, West's argument is that we must exercise judgment on crimes against humanity precisely because we ourselves are prone to committing them.

REBECCA WEST AND THE COLONIALIST HERITAGE

Much about Rebecca West's politics and world view can be explained in terms of her childhood. A radical feminist and socialist, she nevertheless had a strong attachment to the idea of nationhood and even to the British Empire. What makes her essay on Kipling so complex and exquisitely modulated is that she had a foothold in two worlds, the 19th and 20th centuries, the traditionalist and modernist mentalities—a dual consciousness reflected as well in works like Black Lamb and Grey Falcon and the Aubrey Trilogy. I delivered this piece as a paper at an academic conference on colonialism.

The chief tragedy of Rudyard Kipling's life was summed up in two of the tributes published in the newspaper the morning after his death. Major-General Dunsterville, the original of Stalky, boasted: "In three-score years and ten no man's outlook on life could have changed less than that of Rudyard Kipling." Sir Ian Hamilton wrote wisely and powerfully: "As one who must surely be about Kipling's oldest friend, I express my deep sorrow. His death seems to me to place a full stop to the period when war was a romance and the expansion of the Empire a duty." Those two sentences indicate the theme of that tremendous and futile drama in which a man, loving everything in life but reality, spent his days loathing intellectuals as soft and craven theorists, and yet himself never had the courage to face a single fact that disproved the fairy-tales he had invented about the world in youth; and who, nevertheless, was so courageous in defending this uncourageous position that he had to be respected as one respects a fighting bull making its last stand. That drama explains why the public regards Rudyard Kipling as one of the most interesting men of our time. He stands among those Laocoön figures who in pride and strength are treading the road to the highest honours, when they are assailed by passions, which seem not to be a part of the individualities, but to have crawled out of the dark uncharted sea of our common humanity. Such men are judged not by their achievements in action or the arts but by the intensity of the conflict between them and their assailants. Such judgement had to recognize Rudyard Kipling as a memorable man.

Rebecca West published these words in the January 25, 1936, issue of the *New Statesman*. Her essay was later reprinted in *Rebecca West: A Celebration* (1977), a collection that includes some of her best work. Her comments on Kipling are indeed representative of her singular mind and provocative prose. Born in 1892, she emerged out of the Victorian and Edwardian ages to become a modernist writer of fiction, biography, criticism, history, and journalism of a very high order. She allied herself with the Leftist intellectual class that Kipling despised, but she also entertained profoundly conservative sentiments both absorbed during her upbringing and stimulated by her disappointment in a Left that failed to replace Kipling's reactionary vision with a realistic progressivism. West uses the term "reality" in her valedictory to Kipling; I shall return to that term after setting out the terms of her attitude toward the Colonialist heritage.

If the aim of this session is to "probe the subjectivity and subject formation of the colonizers, those whose project depended upon their ability to deny the full humanity and reality of other human beings," then I submit that Rebecca West demands our full attention. She was the daughter of a conservative Anglo-Irish journalist father and a Scottish mother of outstanding musical ability. West was just old enough to remember soldiers returning from the Boer War. Her father's brother, Edward Fairfield, a Colonial Office administrator, was made a scapegoat for the abortive, unauthorized Jameson Raid (December 29, 1895), a foray made by volunteers in to the Boer colony of Transvaal, led by Sir Leander Starr Jameson. Edward Fairfield was charged with sending the Colonial Office approval for the raid. In fact, he condemned it as "unlawful and inexpedient." He never recovered from the accusation and died shortly afterwards. West witnessed her father's grief over this unjust end to his brother's life. This incident, like the Dreyfus Affair, colored West's attitude toward power and colonial governments.

Indeed, West's early career was as a militant feminist and Fabian socialist. Even more importantly, however, she was a radical democrat who warned in 1917—even before the Russian Revolution had ended—that Soviet-style socialism would result in tyranny. She thought as much because she had observed Russian radicals arguing with her father in their London home. Their erratic, often irrational and dictatorial temper, disgusted her and would later become the subject of her greatest novel, *The Birds Fall Down*. By the age of five, she knew what words like communism and socialism and conservatism meant. She had not only her father and mother to tutor her but two older sisters—one a promising poet, the other a political and social activist who would earn degrees in medicine and the law and become an important figure in the London County Council.

Like her sisters, West revolted against her father's anti-feminist, conservative strain, and yet she retained—as did her sisters—a feeling that Colonialism and Progressivism were not always antithetical ideas. She was just old enough to remember Queen Victoria's Diamond Jubilee and the turn of the century "fame of Mr. Kipling." Kipling and the Empire represented "colour"—that is vibrancy and "geographical scope," West remembered. Speaking of the Jubilee and the Diamond Jubilee, West emphasized:

> I do not find that the post-war generation realizes what marvellous shows these were, or how they enfranchised the taste for gorgeousness in a popula-tion that wore dark clothes, partly from a morbid conception of decorum and partly because cleaning was so expensive, and lived in drab and smoky times…. London was full of dark men from the ends of the earth who wore glorious colours and carried strange weapons, and who were all fond of small children and smiled at them in the streets. I remember still with a pang of ecstasy the gleaming teeth of a tall bearded warrior wearing a high head-dress, gold ear-rings and necklaces, a richly muti-coloured uniform, and embroi-dered soft leather boots. There were also the Indian troops in Bushey Park, their officers exquisitely brown and still, and coiffed with delicately bright tur-bans, the men washing their clothes at some stretch of water, small and precise and beautiful. They came from remote places and spoke unknown tongues. They belonged to our Empire, we had helped them to become amiable by conquering them and civilizing them. It was an intoxicating thought; and it was mirrored in the work of Rudyard Kipling and nowhere else, for nobody could match his gift of reflecting visual impressions in his prose, and he alone among professional writers had travelled widely, and had the trick of condens-ing his travels into evocative runes which are almost as much magic as poetry. Hence he could restore confidence to a population that had slowly lost touch with their traditional assurances throughout the nineteenth century and given them a new sense of religious destiny. Since they were subjects of the British Empire they were members of a vast redemptory force.

I quote West at length because there is no other way to show how she combines a feel for the psychology of the colonial imagination, the history of nineteenth-cen-tury Britain, and an evocation of her own childhood and time, with a novelist's grasp of imagery and of telling detail. Phrases such as "enfranchised the taste for gorgeousness" makes of the Diamond Jubilee an event that entitled people to cel-ebrate, making them feel as though they had voted for Empire. Similarly, the yoking of civilization and conquest which becomes an "intoxicating thought," is West's way of demonstrating how ordinary people became drunk on empire.[1] With her quick reference to a nineteenth century that had eroded traditional religious belief and her ringing claim that the "subjects of the British Empire…were members of a vast redemptory force" she powerfully sums up how the Colonialist mentality infected not only the society's leaders but what she calls the "slaves of a mechanized world" who thought it was their "religious destiny" (her words) to bring order back to a "disorganized world."

Thus West probes the "subjectivity and subject formation of the colonizers," revealing Colonialism not as merely a rationale for the subjugation of other peoples but as an intense form of belief that transforms the believer. West understood that without giving Colonialism its due, it is impossible to understand why it flourished and why it floundered. Like any idea, Colonialism both reflects and deflects reality. The reality, as West recognizes in the first paragraph of her Kipling memorial, is that war is not a romance and serving the Empire was not a duty—at least neither the romance nor the duty could be sustained, since both were founded on the claim of one people to dominate other peoples.

Colonialism as a form of enslavement—at home and abroad—becomes the burden of West's essay. If Kipling and the Colonialist imagination energized the British people, both the man and the idea ultimately cut off the British people from reality. Kipling could not change. He continued to believe in the fairy tale of empire, in the "world of youth." West condemns him for this uncourageous behavior. Yet she goes on to state a paradox: respecting him for his courage in "defending this uncourageous position." He is the bull of the British Empire making a last stand. He fights for a dying era.

Kipling is a "memorable man" because his struggle represented forces greater than himself, forces that seemed to have "crawled out of the uncharted sea of our common humanity." Finally, it was Kipling's agonizing struggle with a changing world that makes him a Laocoon figure. In this image of Kipling as Laocoon the writer and the Colonialist heritage are viewed from a broader, more universal perspective. Like Laocoon, West writes, Kipling and other "such men are judged not by their achievements in action or the arts but by the intensity of the conflict between them and their assailants."

West's essay on Kipling does not explicitly concern the question of how to understand the Colonialist heritage, yet her method proves to be a kind of primer embodying precisely the quest to "probe the subjectivity and subjective formation of the colonizers." Ironically, West is able to restore to Kipling the full humanity and reality his life and work sought to deny in others.

---

1.   For another example of West's evocation of empire, see my review of *Survivors in Mexico*, which immediately follows this essay.

Lord Birkenhead, one of Kipling's biographers, observes that Kipling ceased to grow as a writer as soon as he concluded (at a very young age) that he had seen the world. In a final irony, West concludes her essay on Kipling by noting that he had "feared and loathed the aeroplane. Perhaps he felt that, had he given his passion for machinery its head, that and the rest of his creed might have led him straight to Dneprostroi.[2]

---

2.   A hydroelectic station in the central Ukraine. The dam at Dneprostroi was built between 1927 and 1932. It became one of Stalin's much touted achievements.

SURVIVORS IN MEXICO

This review first appeared in The New York Sun. With few exceptions, the reception accorded this posthumous work has been rousing and presages, I hope, a revival of interest in West's work.

The publication of *Survivors in Mexico* is a remarkable event not only for readers of Rebecca West but also for anyone interested in the canon of modern literature. When I read the multiple, incomplete drafts of this book in the West archive at the University of Tulsa, I realized West was writing at the peak of her powers and producing a work that she expected would equal in scope and style her masterpiece, *Black Lamb and Grey Falcon*. I did not think, however, that anyone would be able to assemble a publishable text, since West left so many different versions of her work-in-progress. In *Rebecca West: A Saga of the Century*, I called her book a "truncated masterpiece."

I was wrong. Professor Bernard Schweizer has proven himself to be a brilliant literary detective and an astute editor. He has managed to knit together a text that is faithful to the "fair copy" West left of her work, while also including an introduction and an apparatus of notes at the end of the book, so that those interested in understanding the editorial choices he made can appraise his own interventions.

There are surprises in this book—even for devoted Rebecca West readers. If *Black Lamb and Grey Falcon* attacks the failure of liberals in the 1930s to effectively oppose fascism, and broods on the destructive element in human nature, *Survivors in Mexico*—as its title suggests—affirms her faith that goodness—however it is perverted—can prevail. Readers who turned against West in the 1950s because of her virulent anti-Communism will have to ponder her chapters on figures like Leon Trotsky and Diego Rivera, two of the great heroes of West's epic study of the Aztecs, the Spanish Conquest, and what modern Mexico has become—not only to itself but to the world.

Like *Black Lamb and Grey Falcon*, *Survivors in Mexico* is an amalgam of reportage, autobiography, history, biography, art criticism, poetry, and philosophy. When she describes a Mexico City sunset, it is as if she has seen all the really good ones in the world:

Only here does it seem that the skies go on fire as solid objects do, as if their ashes might rain down on the spectators. Then the mountains were black against crimson, and the crimson marched on and on until it was overhead, and then purple clouds rushed from horizon to horizon, fusing with the crimson and dissolving to rose veils floating on a mulberry firmament, which then was bleached, but brightly, into a greenish crystal arch traversed by white phantoms of mist through which shone stars larger than they had been last week in New York. Lights twinkled up at them from the city below, and it was full night. The operation had taken twenty-five minutes.

Survivors in Mexico is also the emanation of a comic genius. Discussing the cramped conditions in Mexico City, she asks: "How does one make love here without being congratulated by the neighbours in the morning? How can one groan as one dies without making public one's private death, like a poor lost French king? How does one have diarrhoea and got to the bathroom in the night without virtually nationalizing one's intestines?" Her openness to other cultures is balanced by the traveler's inevitable unease in the midst of the unfamiliar, the incomprehensible, and the absurd.

West is a master of digression—the generality that puts her sources—the so-called experts and authorities—in their place. When tackling the issue of foreign investment in Mexico, she divagates: "economists are like Aeolian harps, and the sounds that issue from them are determined by the winds that blow." Describing traffic patterns in Mexico City, she invents "West's law": "once man has invented the internal combustion engine and succeeded in making automobiles at a price which makes it possible for enough of the community to purchase them and for the manufacturer to earn a reasonable profit, then at all times when the purchasers of such vehicles feel the need to use their automobiles they will be unable to proceed at a speed as great as that attained by vehicles before the internal combustion engine was invented." Even better is her explanation of lying: "the lie tampers with fact and produces an illusion that we live in a universe which is not rigid, which can be adjusted to suit our needs."

West was in her seventies when she began her book, and she was entering a period, which, for many reasons, led her to abandon several fictional and nonfictional projects. If she had lost the "finishing power"—as she called it—she still retained her genius to entertain and to instruct in every sentence. The sheer joy of writing up the world is what comes through—as well as a woman still loyal to her radical roots in ways her readers still have not fully appreciated.

This book should help to re-orient not merely perceptions of her career but, I hope, the contemporary discussion of war and peace. She has much to say about both the positive and negative consequences of invasions and occupations. In her view, although much can be said against conquerors like Cortes, in the end she affirms his intervention into the history of Mesoamerica just as much as she approves of Trotsky's residence in Mexico. Both the left and right in this country have much to learn from her. She rejects the idea that cultures can ever really understand each other, although she herself demonstrates a strenuous effort to fathom what is alien to her. Individuals fare no better with each other. Thus she tells the story of her fanatically religious grandmother who never realized a French anarchist was tutoring her sons.

West finds history to be as much comedy as tragedy. The sons got a good education. Mexico benefited greatly from the Spanish Conquest. "We develop," West says at her iconoclastic best, "by misunderstanding"

HISTORY BROUGHT HOME: REBECCA WEST'S YUGOSLAV JOURNEY

This piece originally appeared in the Bangkok Post.

In much of the writing on the conflict in the former Yugoslavia, one title has stood out in recommendations for background reading: *Black Lamb and Grey Falcon* (1941). Its author, Rebecca West (1892-1983), is one of the great writers of the twentieth century. A novelist, biographer, literary critic, and journalist, an early feminist, and staunch anti-Communist, both her fiction and nonfiction exude the stuff of history: revolution, espionage, and war crimes. Her study of the post World War II treason trials, *The Meaning of Treason*, is considered a classic. In its largest sense, all her work is about the shaping of the twentieth century, seen through the eyes of an Englishwoman—as she refers to herself in *Black Lamb and Grey Falcon*. It is, paradoxically, this very personal and yet historical voice that makes her unique and still relevant. She is not afraid to speak for herself and for history. Few writers would approach Yugoslavia—or any other subject for that matter—daring to assume that kind of authority.

To West, what occurs on the world stage must be connected to the private heart. Indeed she layers her narrative with complex psychological and philosophical insights while reminding her readers that it is a journey—a very careful recording of what she saw in Yugoslavia but also a sojourn into the mind of Rebecca West. Autobiography, feminist polemic, history, reportage—*Black Lamb and Grey Falcon* is so many things, not the least of which is an account of how Europe had come to suffer its Second World War, for during the years (1937-1941) she planned, wrote, and published her book, West had to incorporate her reactions to the triumphs of fascism even as her own country and most of Europe remained supine. What accounted for this passivity? she wanted to know.

In Macedonia, in a sheep's field, West witnesses the sacrifice of a black lamb. Disgusted at the sight of the greasy and blood-drenched rock, reeking with the guts of life, she recognizes a ritual meant to purge people of sin. A little girl is brought to watch a man slit the black lamb's throat, catching in the spurt of blood enough to make a circle on the child's forehead. West rejects this shameful ceremony, and the idea that such sacrifice is necessary. She is especially enraged that the little girl will be brought up to believe that such cruelty is required and would associate the very act of child bearing with sin and pain.

Life divides for West right then between people who embrace and reject this notion of sacrifice, which she links to the great Serbian poem (recited to her by Constantine, her Yugoslavian companion) about Tsar Lazar who is visited by a grey falcon (Saint Elijah) offering him the choice of two kingdoms: heaven and earth. Lazar chooses heaven (eternal salvation) rather than earth and accepts the sacrifice of his soldiers and his kingdom in the battle against the Turks. Lazar's choice is the desire to be pure, to make a sacrifice of oneself, rather than be implicated in evil. West rejects the thesis of the poem, that Lazar could redeem himself without considering the fate of his people, for his redemption meant five hundred years of domination by the Turks. In her own time, appeasing Hitler, not fighting meant consigning millions of people to miserable slavery.

West's profound personal and intellectual insight is strengthened by her observation of Constantine, a Yugoslav poet, government official, and a Jew who shepherds her and her husband, Henry Andrews, throughout their trip. Constantine has not merely recited the poem of the grey falcon, he has lived its message, marrying Gerda, a German woman (West's nemesis for most of her trip), and binding his loving heart to this woman of hate so that he might be defeated and innocent. Constantine and Gerda, in fact, suggest the alternative to Rebecca and Henry. Whereas the latter couple are complimented many times on their compatibility (they provide pleasure for one party who observes how close they sit together even though they are not young), the former are the very epitome of the forces rending Europe apart. Watching what West calls beautiful Macedonian boys and girls dancing in the open air with clothes as lovely as flowers, Gerda takes out a cigarette and declares that she must smoke to disinfect herself, for she feels contaminated by people she does not consider civilized Europeans. Gerda see no order or culture but only a mish-mash of different and primitive peoples.

Rebecca West's journey through Yugoslavia is still relevant because of the questions she posed. Is such cruelty necessary? Why hasn't it been stopped? Why does the world seem so helpless, so supine in the face of obvious evil that has been spreading in the heart of Europe? She would have been especially appalled at the destruction of Sarajevo, a city of such rich ethnicity and cosmopolitanism, which stood as the very type of what a civilization should be. That such a city should be shelled into oblivion would surely have caused her to cry out that the world itself had been dealt a crippling blow. What happens there—in Sarajevo—she would say, will also happen here—in your own heart; the world is a little less safe for a diverse humanity. The price paid for not making Yugoslavia our problem has done untold damage, which writers of the next generation will spend precious time accounting for.

I tried to explain all of this to Amelia, my sixteen-year-old daughter, as we drove to a suburb of Washington, D.C., where I was to interview the sisters Gavrilovic, the daughters of Milan Gavrilovic, the head of the Serbian Peasant Party in Yugoslavia and a member of the Yugoslav government-in-exile in London during World War II. Milan Gavrilovic had met Rebecca West in London and lauded her masterpiece on his country; his daughters had become her friends. It was an extraordinary evening of reminiscences, but not a word was said about what is happening today in Yugoslavia. Finally, I broached the delicate topic. Almost as a chorus the sisters exclaimed it was too painful to discuss.

Just as my daughter and I were preparing to leave, a young woman entered the house. We were introduced. As I was making my goodbyes, my daughter sat with her in the kitchen talking. It was late. We had to go. There was no way to reopen the subject, which would have been like re-opening wounds. I never even learned whether this young woman, a Bosnian, was a Serb, or would have identified herself as such. What struck me is that she had made a journey; we had made a journey. There was still so much to learn, and my daughter seemed exhilarated. She had come not knowing what to expect, with only the vaguest sense of the history her father had tried to communicate to her. But something personal had been sparked in her during that evening, ratifying what Rebecca West's great twentieth century book calls on all of us to do—to bring history home and make it our own.

Postscript

I often wondered if that evening with the Gavrilovics made as much of an impact on them as it had on me. Then nearly a decade later, I received an email from Kosara Gavrilovic:

Dear Carl,

It has been a long time since our last contact…. Lately you have been much present in Aleksa's [her brother's] and my thoughts because we are writing a book about our father and are just now putting finishing touches on the chapter about Rebecca's friendship with our parents. We were hunting for dates of some of her publications, and your book was a godsend. Of course, I could have gone to the Library of Congress and looked it all up there, but now that I am almost 81 I do not relish looking for parking spaces on Capitol Hill. This last weekend I was at Soza's [her sister's] and we reminisced about the very enjoyable dinner at her house with you and your charming daughter.... I...would still like to send you my book...some translations, I think, are quite successful and might have met with Rebecca's approval had she lived to read them.

With best regards, yours

Kosara Gavrilovic

REBECCA WEST, THE WEST, AND THE LEGACY OF BLACK LAMB AND GREY FALCON

I delivered this talk as the Sydney Rosenberg Memorial Lecture at Kingsborough Community College, on Tuesday, November 9, 1999

Journalist Bernard Levin called Rebecca West one of the greatest women in the history of Western civilization, comparing her to Elizabeth I, no less, in suggesting the magnitude of West's achievement. Yet I feel the need to re-introduce West every time I write or speak about her. She was a prophet, and in her most prophetic of books, *Black Lamb and Grey Falcon,* she predicted her own fate. She was, she wrote, doomed to fade in and out of public consciousness because she never stuck to one thing: she was a biographer, a historian, a novelist, a journalist, a travel writer, an esthetician, a literary critic—and she often combined these roles in books like *Black Lamb and Grey Falcon*, which Truman Capote hailed as a precursor of the nonfiction novel. If West has not ascended to the literary pantheon—at least not yet—she returns, again and again, refusing to be repressed. I completed my biography of her in 1995; nevertheless, she refuses to let go of me. This is an alarming if also an intriguing case of being haunted by a subject. I have gone on to other work, but with each passing day, each world crisis or development, I keep asking myself "What would Rebecca West have thought?" Of course, the clearest instance of her presence is the current concern over the fate of the former Yugoslavia. In a new book, *Kosovo Crossing* (1999), David Fromkin writes:

> When we want to have an elucidation of any number of issues regarding Yugoslavia and its impact on great power politics, it is remarkable how often we find that West has been there before us. Indeed, as we enter the twenty-first century, we seem to cross the path of Rebecca West all the time.

Fromkin is referring not merely to West's vision of history but to her reporter's eye for events. He cites, for example, her account of the Nuremberg trials, an account which has never been bettered and which is relevant today, needless to say, in the discussions of war crimes, crimes against humanity, and international tribunals. One could go on and on praising West's achievements—noting her brilliant coverage of a lynching trial in South Carolina, her biography of the traitor William Joyce—not to mention extraordinary novels like *The Return of the Soldier* and *The Birds Fall Down*, imaginative works that explore the causes and consequences of World War I and the Russian Revolution. As befits her name, Rebecca West took as her province the whole of Western history and that history's impact on the world.

How Rebecca West got to be Rebecca West is, of course, part of the story of why we value her today, and of why she is also neglected or attacked—for like most prophets she has been both honored and vilified. Her truths are uncomfortable truths—as I will try to show later when I consider other, less positive responses to *Black Lamb and Grey Falcon*. She believed that she would be persecuted for what she had to say. There was, in fact, another actual Rebecca West, a 17th century English woman who was hanged as a witch. Her twentieth-century namesake said her books did not receive reviews but maledictions.

Rebecca West, the author, was born Cicily Fairfield in London on December 21, 1892. Her father was an Anglo-Irish journalist and her Scottish mother an accomplished pianist who did not pursue a professional career. Both parents were highly articulate and as interested in politics as in art. Cicily—or Cissie, as the family called her—was a precocious toddler who tried to keep up with her older sisters, one of whom became a poet and the other a doctor and lawyer. Cissie absorbed, it seems, every word of the conversations between her parents and their visitors, many of whom were interesting types her father brought home. By the age of five, Cissie knew about Russian revolutionaries because she had met them in her father's company.

Cissie loved the theater, adored Sarah Bernhardt, and wanted to become an actress. But she was short, dark featured and apparently something of an unruly student in drama school, criticizing her teachers for choosing plays of poor quality. She took the name Rebecca West from a character in an Ibsen play, *Rosmersholm,* which features an outspoken woman who feels ostracized by society. Rebecca West was a pen, not a stage name, taken when Cissie realized that her radical feminist writing, which she began to publish before she was nineteen, disturbed her mother. It was not so much that what Cissie said was wrong but that her way of saying it drew attention to herself. In short, Rebecca West would always be an actress and would treat world history as her stage.

There are writers who merely wish to record what they see, and then there are writers who strive to impress what they see on the world. Rebecca West was of the latter category, taking her cues from writers such as D. H. Lawrence, another traveler and prophet of modern consciousness, and from H. G. Wells, with whom she had a rocky ten-year relationship which produced a son, the writer Anthony West. Like her other roles, motherhood suited West only fitfully, and her quarrels with Anthony would become an epic subject for her. The note of family discord—West's father abandoned the family when she was five—sounds throughout her work. She lived in the world of King Lear, in a kingdom gone awry, and it was to King Lear she would constantly revert in her greatest work, Black Lamb and Grey Falcon.

Although Rebecca West was made a Dame of the British Empire in 1958, she never felt quite at home in England—or anywhere else, for that matter. She was for one thing a fault finder. As one wag put it in the British journal Time and Tide:

> It is probable that if there is ever an English Revolution there will come a point when the Reds and Whites will sink their differences for ten minutes while they guillotine Miss West for making remarks that both sides have found intolerably unhelpful.

She traveled in order to find a spiritual home. She found America very appealing but could not live in a republic. Progressive on many fronts, she nevertheless supported the British monarchy. She found Mexico dazzling and planned a book that would have rivaled Black Lamb and Grey Falcon if she had found the stamina in her later years to complete it. But it was Yugoslavia that came closest to the heaven of her desires.

The kingdom of the South Slavs, which is what Yugoslavia means, was a polyglot culture that appealed to a woman who called herself a Celt. It had a wonderful history of dynasties with great kings and a tragic destiny, the Serb defeat at Kosovo in 1389, which led to centuries of Turkish dominance in the region. Always pro-Western, no matter how severely she criticized her own culture, West would today be deemed politically incorrect. Indeed, she was prejudiced against the Turks. In a draft of her book on Mexico, she argued that it was a good thing that Europeans conquered the New World. How would it look for a continent stretching from Mexico to Canada to have the fez as its dominant headgear? Is it still permissible to laugh at such questions? Or have we become so concerned about tolerance that our visceral reactions to cultural differences must be carefully subdued? Well, West thought the fez look silly.

In her own day, the issues were not political correctness and multicuturalism but internationalism and nationalism. Nationalism was often equated with narrow mindedness and bigotry. Better to cleanse the world of ethnic differences and religious distinctions; better to count on the bright future of the Soviet Union. West thought this kind of internationalism naive and dangerous. She did not want to obliterate differences. She thought each nation should take pride in its identity while recognizing that its values, if imposed on other nations, would be tyranny. The world, in other words, should not become more like the Soviet Union or Great Britain; rather, each country should celebrate its own unique contribution to civilization. To her everlasting dismay, she saw the Left in Britain and many of her friends in the Labor Party defer to the Soviet Union as a vanguard political culture. The result, in her view, was a degradation of British politics and specifically the destruction of the idea of socialism.

West turned toward Yugoslavia because she felt it embodied older Western values The Serbs never forgot the lesson of defeat at Kosovo. Legend had it that Saint Elijah appeared in the form of a grey falcon to Lazar, the Serb prince, and offered Lazar a choice: victory at Kosovo and a triumphant reign in this world, or defeat at Kosovo but everlasting life and salvation. By choosing the latter, Lazar consigned his people to centuries of suffering. The idea that one should sacrifice oneself or others in order to obtain peace was anathema to West. She had in mind, of course, Neville Chamberlain's capitulation to Adolf Hitler at Munich, a capitulation that was the culmination of nearly a decade of appeasement. What infuriated and saddened West was that her countrymen—many of her best friends, in fact—initially responded to Munich as a victory ("peace in our time"). Unlike the Serbs, who had never gotten over their defeat in 1389, the British did not even realize they were defeated, that they had sacrificed the Czechs to Nazi rule. West gave her heart to a people for whom 1389 and 1939 were no further apart than yesterday and today. History was brought home to Serbs every day and finally by the early 20th century they had managed to free themselves of both the Turks and the Habsburg monarchy. Writing *Black Lamb and Grey Falcon* in the years leading up to World War II, West was aghast that her countrymen seemed quite willing to make the Serbs the next gift to Hitler, although the Serbs, even after their defeat in 1389, resisted the encroaching Turks and protected the gates, so to speak, of Western civilization. Her own countryman believed that somehow this sacrifice, like the sacrifice of a black lamb she had witnessed in Yugoslavia, would guarantee their own survival. It was an ugly, revolting doctrine, making other creatures atone for one's sins.

West's attack on the atonement occurs during a tour of the countryside as she approaches a Sheep's field. The sacrifice of a lamb on a slimy rock appalls West. That out of this disgusting ceremony of bloodletting a woman will supposedly become fruitful seems to sum up the perverted nature of human beings who believe that salvation can be attained only through suffering. An outraged West exclaims:

> Women do not get children by adding to the normal act of copulation the slaughter of a lamb, the breaking of a jar, the decapitation of a cock, the stretching of wool through blood and grease. If there was a woman whose womb could be unsealed by witnessing a petty and pointless act of violence, by seeing a jet of blood fall from a lamb's throat on a rock wet with stale and stinking blood, her fertility would be the reverse of motherhood, she would have children for the purpose of hating them....

To move from this scene at the rock to a consideration of genocide, the "ethnic cleansing" of the new Balkan Wars is also to enter the most controversial part of West's legacy. What would she have thought of the Serbs today? What would she say about what has happened in the former Yugoslavia? I am not one of those biographers who claims to enter his subject's minds, or who has dreams in which his subjects speak to him. But I can sketch out some of the lines of West's reply, especially since I do know that she continued to think and speak about Yugoslavia right up to 1983, the year of her death.

To West, the Serbs had taken the lead in creating the new Yugoslavia that emerged out of World War I. She did not deny the heavy-handed Serb dominance over the Croats and the Muslims. But as she pointed out in *Black Lamb and Grey Falcon*, there were no ethnic differences between the three groups, and the Serbs saw most clearly why as Slavs they should unite. Croats, on the other hand, had been much closer to the Habsburgs and to Germany, seeing less clearly what it meant to be independent Slavs. Muslims were caught in the middle, as they are today, and West did not see how they could maintain a Bosnian identity except as a part of Yugoslavia.

For all her brilliant writing about Yugoslavia, West's vision of the Serbs, according to some commentators, seems irrelevant, if not pernicious in light of what is happening today. In his well received book, *Slaughterhouse: Bosnia and the*

Failure of the West (1995), David Rieff mentions West as the author of one of the "great travel books of the interwar period," but then he demurs:

> For all her originality, West, in her famous book, was very much a writer of her times. However much she hated German "race thinking" she herself was unable to make sense of much of what she saw during her six weeks in Yugoslavia without appeal to explanations based on the array of supposedly immutable "national characteristics" that she believed to apply to the individual Serbs, Croats, Muslims, and Germans she encountered.

I suppose West would reply, "Do you mean to say there is no such thing as national characteristics?" While history is a record of change, it can also be a record of continuity, of characteristics that persist. Rieff is very much the kind of internationalist that West criticized. He is pro-Muslim because he believes that Sarajevo embodied a multicultural, internationalist ideal, one that the Serbs dismembered when they made a slaughterhouse of Bosnia. For Rieff, as for his mother Susan Sontag, sentimentalizing Sarajevo is a way to relive the internationalist camaraderie the Left experienced during the Spanish Civil War.

West would surely point out that the tragedy of Serb nationalism is that Slobodan Milosevic, a corrupt leader tutored in the Tito tradition, has commandeered it. West despised Tito precisely because he did not solve the problems of tensions between Croats, Muslims, and Serbs; he simply repressed them. He tried to impose the ideology of Communism on all Slavs even as the wounds of World War II festered. In Tito's Yugoslavia, it was not important to identify oneself as Serb, Croat, or Muslim. But this strategy of denying or blurring distinctions, of reconciling but not erasing differences, simply postponed the day of reckoning. Even before Tito died, signs of decay were evident. Franjo Tudjman, now Croatia's fascist dictator, was agitating for Croatian independence. In response, Tito tried to work out a system giving more autonomy to the country's republics. But how could a country survive on a bankrupt ideology—one that was shown to be a sham in the countries neighboring Yugoslavia?

In the late 1980s, after Tito's death, Milosevic latched on to the issue of Kosovo, of preserving the Serbs' historic identity. For more than four decades, Serbs, Croats, and Muslims had virtually no experience of dealing with each other as Serbs, Croats, and Muslims. All they hand, in a sense, was their historic memory, one that had been frozen in 1945, when Tito took control of the whole country and shortly thereafter executed his Serb rival, General Mihailovich.

I have been reprising rather baldly a good deal of the ground West covered in postwar debates about the fate of Yugoslavia and the spread of Communism. So far I have extrapolated very little. Now I will have to extend what West said in order to reply to her critics and to suggest what the legacy of her great book is and how it might serve as a primer for the future.

I do not see how West could do other than condemn today's Serb leaders. They are simply Communist thugs who have re-engineered themselves. Yet how could she abandon the Serbs? As bad as the Milosevic regime is, Tudjman in Croatia is worse. Even a writer as anti-Serb and pro-Muslim as Susan Sontag has said as much. The Muslims are not numerous enough to take the lead in a regional solution to the breakup of Yugoslavia. Only the Serbs, with substantial populations in most of the former Yugoslav republics, have the capacity, geographically and historically, to establish the peace.

That is quite a thing to say given the odious picture of the Serbs presented in the Western press. But to suppose that the Serbs could once again take the lead in the former Yugoslavia is not much more unthinkable than the idea that Germans would be able to reunite after decades of division. It is no more unthinkable than that one day the British hailed Chamberlain as their savior and the next discarded him for Churchill—until then one of the great failures of British politics.

West wrote an Epilogue to *Black Lamb and Grey Falcon* after World War II began, expressing her relief and pride that British appeasement had been transformed into British indomitability. That epilogue has to be kept in mind, for it counteracts the idea that her book simply endorses the vision of Yugoslavia as a land of ancient hatreds and bitter blood feuds. In a misguided *New Yorker* article (April 15, 1996), Brian Hall, author of a respected book on Yugoslavia, attacked a rival, Robert Kaplan, for elevating West into a dangerous position of authority. In *Balkan Ghosts* (1993), Kaplan writes: "I would rather have lost my passport and money than my heavily thumbed and annotated copy of 'Black Lamb and Grey Falcon.'" Like West, Hall argues, Kaplan believes in "national essences." A sense of fatality and doom mark Kaplan's narrative, which, Hall insists "emulates West." Hall calls Kaplan's book a self-fulfilling story which lends a plot to history when history cannot be altered. For Hall, it is a short step from West, to Kaplan, to Clinton's fatal inaction over many years. Why intervene when the Balkans have always been a hopeless cause?

Hall was writing before Clinton finally did intervene—very late in the day, just as Britain waited until after the shame of Munich and the invasion of Poland to go to war. I wonder if West—so fond of finding historical analogues—would have latched on to this one. So many times the West has been found wanting, has been considered weak, and yet history has its epilogue as well as its prologue. If for Rebecca West history is fated—like Lazar's decision at Kosovo—that fate was only determined at the moment of decision, and the moment of decision is always now. If 1389 largely determined what was still happening in 1939, then the reverse was also true: what was yet to happen in 1939 could change the ultimate significance of what happened in 1389.

To write off the Serbs, to write off the West, to write off Rebecca West is not possible. She was an essentialist who paradoxically saw essence evolving out of existence. It is a travesty to suggest that her views would condone inaction, a simple giving into fate. But fate hovers over West"s world as powerfully as it does in many great works of literature, such as *King Lear* and *Beowulf* in which destiny becomes apparent only after the hero has acted.

I cannot extrapolate from West much further, except to say that reading *Black Lamb and Grey Falcon* raises questions that both foretell and forestall our fate, questions that leave history open-ended. Even though so many episodes in West's work result in human defeat, the sheer narrative drive of *Black Lamb and Grey Falcon* triumphs and constitutes—to adapt a phrase from D. H. Lawrence—"the bright book of life."

REBECCA WEST'S RELIGIOUS QUEST

Shortly after my biography of Rebecca West was published, John Wilson, editor of a new periodical, Books and Culture, sponsored by Christianity Today, asked me to write a piece about West's religious beliefs. I found it impossible to write a single coherent account and took refuge in the following notes, which he did not deem publishable. I cannot say that he was wrong, but as a series of notes, the following may at least provoke more discussion about the vexed question of what West believed. For readers especially concerned with West's religious ideas and her attitude toward religion, I direct them to the work of Bernard Schweizer, the world authority on her religious quest and to the forthcoming iUniverse collection of West's essays, Woman as Artist and Thinker.

1. May 3, 1938. The Sacrifice at the Stone

On her third trip to Yugoslavia, Rebecca West finally found the climatic scene of *Black Lamb and Grey Falcon*, rightly called "one of the great books of spiritual revolt" in the twentieth century. In Macedonia, her car left the road and ploughed part-way through a pasture until she had to get out and walk the remaining distance to the rock, a level mound standing about six feet high, red-brown and gleaming with the blood of sacrificed beasts. West had to thread her way through a disgusting scene of bleeding cocks' heads, and men, women, and children, sitting and lying at the base of the stone. In the putrid air, she scanned the rock stuck with greasy candles and strands of wool, dyed red and pink, and pronounced her anathema on it:

> It would have been pleasant to turn round and run back to the car and drive away as quickly as possible, but the place had enormous authority. It was the body of our death, it was the seed of the sin that is in us, it was the forge where the sword was wrought that shall slay us.

To West, this desolate scene reflected not only the human fascination with death and sacrifice, but with the idea of atonement—that somehow through a bloodbath, sin could be cleansed; life could be renewed. She had sought a way to absolve sin and to welcome salvation—but not this way, she protested, repulsed at a conception of religion that required such abasement of the human spirit.

In West's day, Yugoslavia seemed the place for her quest—much as it is today for Susan Sontag, who has gone back to Sarajevo again and again—nine times in all—to find truth in a form that is purer than what West called the "diffused life" of Western cities. West's quest, like Sontag's, has an element of the pastoral, a yearning to be saved by a people and place that seem more sinned against than sinning, but who are caught up in the war of the human spirit, in a kind of Man-ichean drama that troubled West's great hero, St. Augustine, the subject of her penetrating biography.

At the rock an elegant, immaculately dressed man with dark golden skin, looking like an Indian prince, walked a circle around the rock and stooped to kiss its bloody surface. He lifted a lamb to the edge of the rock, and with a knife slit its throat, making with its blood a circle on a young girl's forehead. He was indeed completing a circle, West was told, because it was at this rock that a sacri-fice had been made for the sake of his wife (barren for fifteen years), who had sub-sequently conceived this child. But to West, this scene became a stench that "mounted more strongly and became sickening."

"It was a huge and dirty lie," she declared, that said of this sacrifice a life would come. This perverted crucifixion scene reminded her of all religions that made a good of Christ's sacrifice rather than seeing it for what it was: the destruction of one who "taught mankind to live in perpetual happiness." Her own theology taught her that Christ stood for the idea of a "universe, half inside and half out-side our minds, which is wholly adorable; and this it was that men killed when they crucified Jesus Christ." West rejected the necessity of suffering and advo-cated hedonism, a belief that only what is pleasant or has pleasant consequences is intrinsically good. It was our duty to promoted a desire for pleasure and to avoid pain. No matter how the established religions dressed it up, no matter how grace-ful the priest—or the man at the rock—the doctrine of atonement that stipulated suffering sickened her.

2. God the Father

Rebecca West had been drawn to the rock as to a revelation, yet she could not accept what she saw. She had been searching for redemption since childhood, ever since her charismatic but wayward father abandoned her mother and her two older two sisters. Precocious Rebecca, only eight years old when her father left home and believing she was his favorite, expressed her loss in a poem about her faithless twin.

In the family romance father rules. To Tony Redd, an American student of Rebecca West's work and her Boswell for a season in the mid 1970s, her version of Father was reminiscent of Piers Aubrey in her autobiographical novel, *The Fountain Overflows*, narrated by his daughter Rose, Rebecca's surrogate. "I had a glorious father. I had no father at all," Rose concludes. Father broods and flares with such intellectual and emotional intensity that the family kindles in his presence. "We are all less than Piers," his wife avows. Aubrey is magnificently aloof, so remote at times that he seems more like a myth than a man: "He walked as if he had no weight, as if no limitation affected him." God the Father.

Rebecca West pondered the meaning of her loss. Why did she have to suffer it? Had it been really necessary? Who could say? By the age of twelve, she was reading Saint Augustine under the tutelage of a Jesuit. Although she was not a Catholic, she powerfully identified with him as a father of the church and treated him much as she treated the memory of her father: by turns reverently and critically, proud of his authority and angry at his human fallibility.

By the 1920s, when she was emerging from her most ardent phase as a socialist and feminist, a thirty-three year old West called Christianity "a phase of revelation," though not the final word. She dismissed the Virgin Birth with an analogy the devout would find flippant, calling it "as absurd as persons would be who, having been visited by the wisest man in the world, stopped repeating his wisdom to an audience longing to hear it and wrangled whether he had travelled to their house by a bus or a tramcar." She found the Atonement a personal affront:

> That a father should invent the laws of a game knowing that they must be broken, force people to play it, sentence the players to punishment for breaking them, and accept the agony of his son as a substitute for the punishment, was credible enough to people who believed that hate might be the ultimate law of life. To us who have been given the Christian idea of love and mercy as an essential part of divinity, it is not credible.

But what was credible baffled Rebecca West. In the 1920s, she indulged in the fad of going to séances and wrote fiction about mediums and fortune tellers, even though she found most practitioners of the occult foolish or fraudulent. Yet she believed in poltergeist all her life, and was only half kidding when she said God did not love women writers. She had trouble not believing in a malign fate.

3. Revelation

By 1933, West had worked out a vision of revelation, writing her testament in the form of a short mock memoir, *A Letter to A Grandfather*, published by Virginia and Leonard Woolf's Hogarth Press. The letter is signed by C.B., the most recent descendant of the Beauchamp family. She has just experienced "my share of the vision that comes to each generation of our family." Exactly what she has seen and what it means is difficult to puzzle out, because it is not really comprehensible in human terms. It is a vision of God; it is "one moment when life was presented to you as a unity," she says to her grandfather, who has experienced his own version of the vision.

C. B. experiences something exactly opposite to the modern notion of self. She contrasts it to buying clothes, which is "so Berkleyan. One wraps the self in gorgeousness as if to say, 'There's nothing but you really, the universe is just a figment you keep on creating, if I give you all these lovely presents will you make me a lovelier universe?'" The religious experience, the abbey that C. B.'s original ancestor built to commemorate his vision, reminds her of the limitations of the self, of its inability to measure the world, to grasp the unity behind appearances: "But a man cannot stretch more than a certain distance from his head and his belly; and that makes him a tense and interesting pattern worked on the surface of infinity." Christ on the cross is an image of that imprisonment in time and place and of a yearning for an experience that transcends the suffering of such limitations. In the abbey, C. B. has seen the dove:

> the thing that flies forth, the *logos*, the symbol of the spirit…the full life of which is lived only by certain human beings, and by certain parts of human beings, which flies forth and pillages the material life with its sharp, greedy beak of criticism, while the natural man stands by and curses, seeing his relationship with his environment ruptured, yet knowing himself under an ineluctable obligation to support the life of the spirit.

In her own family, most of the men have been materialists, men of action, "interrupted only every two hundred years or so by a man of the analytic type who employs artists or is himself an artist." It makes her think of the "Italian philosopher's theory of the human spiral, which implies that man passes through alternate phases of determinism and free will." She is referring to Vico, who has profoundly influenced many modernist writers. As in her family, so in the history of humankind, individuals have been surfeited with experience and have acted almost like automatons, victims of an "obvious determinism." Eventually, however, the overload of experience is inventoried and digested; human beings impose patterns on their behavior, exert, in effect, free will. History, then, is the spiral of these centrifugal and centripetal forces, intersected by the efforts of individuals who at any moment may succumb to or conquer their experiences.

This is a philosophy of history not easily or neatly proven, C.B. concedes, but it has made enormous imaginative sense to artists, and it helps her to account for her family's generation-by-generation visions of the whole, of the unity of experience. Each age, she realizes, has adapted the vision to its temperament, so that, for example, it appears in a rational, ordered form in the eighteenth-century, as a God approximating the guise of a Romantic poet in the nineteenth-century. The varieties of religious experience change but not the "persistence of the life of the spirit." Human beings can kill doves, but not the dove, the Holy Ghost.

A Letter to a Grandfather is an effort to reawaken a sense of the spirit, which has attenuated over the past two centuries. Romanticism emphasized the sensating individual, a necessary phase for humanity to go through in order to have experience to interpret, but by itself romanticism was destructive. West had already argued that romanticism needed classicism, a sense of objective form, to critique it; otherwise all one had was that Berkleyan revelry in solipsism, that clothing of the self. She saw a corrective in the nineteenth century scientist's emphasis on the idea of coherence and on ascertainable fact, for it rooted humanity once more in a quest for the unity of experience.

West had written to novelist Hugh Walpole that in another age she would have looked on herself as one who had sinned against the Holy Ghost. She had in mind her complicity in the human tendency to destroy the unity of experience. She has C. B. say, "I loathe the way the two cancers of sadism and masochism eat into the sexual life of humanity." In West's letters, it was usually her lovers H.G. Wells or newspaper magnate Max Beaverbrook who perpetrated these sins, but what made her so ashamed, is that she had played their game: "My twenties were joyless and overworked and lonely, but this was entirely my own fault. I lost patience with my home life too soon and tried to arrange my life for myself and did it badly."

C. B., like Rebecca West, does not have the consolations that others of their generation turned to in the 1930s, that helped others impose a unity of experience on themselves. Rebecca believed in tradition—as she was to show in her biography of Saint Augustine—but in her time "tradition has been thrown out of the window by all parties, even by those who pretend to be traditionalists," C. B. concludes. The Roman Catholic Church had gained converts who did not believe in revelation, but who disliked the disorder of life without authority.

What authority could the Church have, however, if its basis of authority—revelation—was denied?

A Letter to a Grandfather ends in a dramatic scene—the vision C. B. has had of a tall, gaunt Negro carnival barker on the platform of a merry-go-round composed of miniature automobiles. It is an image of a whirling world—never quite the same at any moment, but all of a piece nevertheless. The Negro calls people to the cars and is immediately aware of the traffic problems they create. As he drives them on with his cane, making sure that the merry-go-round is full, they seem to lose their volition. He uses his cane, in other words, as a shepherd's staff, and he takes the same degree of pleasure and irritation in herding his flock as a shepherd might. Then he holds his cane rigidly on the level, so that it looks like an iron bar, suggesting both discipline and judgment. The merry-go-round revolves, and the barker mesmerizes his audience with a hand trick, thrusting the first finger and thumb of his right hand into a circle he has made out of the first finger and thumb of his left hand. "His teeth shone, his rolling eyeballs exhibited the whites of his eyes; it was as if a gleaming bird, a dove shot forth from his face and in its flight became his finger." It is a cheap trick, a tawdry show. But it delights the crowd as though it were a firework; it is a revelation, an emanation of the spirit.

C. B.'s vision emphasizes that for the human being the true religious experience is likely to be grim, not grand. If the first in her family to have a vision saw a gaunt figure extended on a cross, she has also seen the same thing in the Negro's form; she experiences the same "attempt to cover all, to know all, to feel all, although fixed to one point in the universe, and thereby pinned to ignorance." Advancing a sense of predestination that will be worked out in West biography of St. Augustine, C. B. announces: "I also know that some are born to be saved and some to be damned, that the pulse which is heard through time and space beats to some other rhythm than human justice." The spirit that she sees is not "holy or independent." It is rather the "white product of dark gestures, the refined descendant of man's primitive play." In the Negro's dark gestures and primitive play is found the unity of experience, of Christ on the Cross stretching toward eternity. It is not a pretty or an ennobling vision, but it is a revelation of tragedy that has come back into her life. It is a vision that kindles "the will to belief." C. B. is careful not to say that she believes, merely that the idea of the spirit has been resurrected, and that it brings, she sees, "an inevitable happiness."

4. Original Sin

In *Saint Augustine* (1934), West describes the church father as the great scourge of heresies—not only Manicheanism, but Arianism (that Christ was not divine), Pelagianism (original sin does not obtain and man's will is free to achieve righteousness), and Donatism (only a righteous priest can administer the sacraments). Each heresy struck at the idea that the spirit, the divine principle, was whole and indivisible, above and beyond the limitations of time and place. Augustine countered that the spiritual life had to be a unity of experience; it should not be fragmented by any belief, no matter how consoling or humanly appealing.

Later, in *Black Lamb and Grey Falcon*, West makes explicit the parallel embedded in her biography: "I had written...a life of St. Augustine to find out why every phrase I read of his sounds in my ears like the sentence of my doom and the doom of my age." Her contemporaries were following false gods, thus splitting themselves from a recognition of the spirit, of humanity in its wholeness. Drawn perversely to death-inflicting ideas, she meant to jolt people out of them. West had begun her career in *The Freewoman* (June 6, 1912) dismissing the Calvinism of her native Scotland, deciding that it was "impossible to argue with a person who holds the doctrine of original sin." Her own experience and her reading of history had caused her to recant:

If we examine ourselves carefully we cannot claim to have free will. We

> exercise what looks like a free faculty of choice, but the way we exercise that faculty depends on our innate qualities and our environment, and these always bind us in some way or another to the neuroses which compel us to choose death rather than life. We cannot break this compulsion by the independent efforts of our minds, for they cannot function effectively unless they learn to depend on tradition. Augustine's view that we are full of original sin, that we do not enjoy the free use of our wills, and must link ourselves to the eternal if we are to be saved, is at least a symbolic interpretation of something that the most secular-minded must allow to be true.

Unlike Augustine, West did not work out a theology or embrace the Church (although in the early 1950s she considered following her older sister and converting to Catholicism); even as she entertains Augustine's determinism she shies away from doctrine, calling it only a "symbolic interpretation."

5. Redemption

West lived to be ninety, dying on the ides of March in 1983. She never ceased her quest for revelation; she never quite found it. What is striking in the enormous energy of her religious inquiry. Well into her seventies she was scrambling up Mexican pyramids and Crusader castles in Lebanon, studying Aztec religion and the Druses, fascinated with their confection of Christianity and Islam. She never finished her epic study of Mexico, which would have rivaled her masterpiece on Yugoslavia. She pondered why human beings continued to believe in the necessity of sacrifice.

In Lebanon, she was vouchsafed one more revelation. One day in the desert her driver stopped the car and pointed. At first, it seemed no more than a little whirlwind, a puff of smoke, no, a huge round cobweb, of the same substance as the gossamers that hang on hedges on autumn mornings, but tall as a man. "In Australia, we call them 'Willy-Willies,'" her traveling companion said. West watched the ghostly dance of these skeletal figures. It was difficult not to believe they had emotions, joy or rage, for they moved with seeming purpose like human beings executing a command, grumbling or exalting in it. The pale maroon desert and a huge cumulus cloud cast a shadow over the scene, while the sun appeared a golden bar behind it, falling straight from the heat-bleached blue sky. Five minutes later West saw a giant amber Willy—perhaps thirty feet high—turning and twirling its dancer's body, vanishing and reappearing, apparently in a frenzy, struggling to free its swathed arms, rising from the ground, with a head covered with red gold, curling hair. It pivoted wildly until a long curl whipped out and its feet sank to the earth. This figure keep reconstituting itself, dense and evanescent, like the materialization of a human being, tussling for some knowledge denied it.

Rebecca West always tusseled for the truth, for a vision of the whole. It always eluded her, but she never gave in to a mean spirited sense that there was no meaning. Asked if she believed in an afterlife, she replied: "After all, *this* life is so improbable—why not?"

978-0-595-36227-1
0-595-36227-3

Printed in the United States
152265LV00006B/43/A